Enacting the Work of Language Instruction

HIGH-LEVERAGE TEACHING PRACTICES

VOLUME 2

EILEEN W. GLISAN

RICHARD DONATO

Graphic Design by Paintbox Creative, LLC

Graphic in Figure 4.1, U-Shaped Learning, reprinted from Second Language Acquisition by Susan M. Gass and Larry Selinker with the permission of Taylor and Francis Group LLC Books.

ISBN: 978-1-942544-71-5

1001 North Fairfax Street, Suite 200
Alexandria, VA 22314

ACKNOWLEDGEMENTS

The first volume of *Enacting the Work of Language Instruction: High-Leverage Teaching Practices* was met with overwhelming enthusiasm by language teachers and teacher educators across the country. As a result, the book has been extensively used by pre-service teachers in university practicum courses as well as by in-service teachers in professional development programs. In the first volume, language educators were introduced to the concept of HLTPs and presented with a set of six practices, largely focused on oral interpersonal communication, that are essential for teachers to enact in their classrooms to support second language learning and development. However, our work with students and teachers in classrooms has shown that there are at least four additional practices that address areas not covered in the first volume: a meaningful context for teaching, backward-design planning, purposeful written communication, and contextualized performance assessment. With the addition of these four practices, the field will have a set of ten practices that more fully reflect the minimum expectations for accomplished language teaching. It is our hope that this second volume will be met with the same level of excitement as with the first volume. Further, we hope that it will be used in conjunction with the first volume to mediate initial teacher training and ongoing professional development and as a way to continue the robust dialogue among language professionals regarding HLTPs.

We recognize the voices of our students, graduates of the teacher preparation programs at our respective institutions, our colleagues, our publisher, and our reviewers in the work that resulted in this second volume. To this end, we acknowledge the support and enthusiasm of Howie Berman, Executive Director of ACTFL, as well as the ACTFL Board of Directors, throughout the writing and production of this volume. We also thank Marty Abbott, whose encouragement when conceptualizing the first volume sustained our efforts through the completion of this two-volume series. We are grateful to the production team at ACTFL, specifically Sherri Halloran, Marketing and Communications Manager, whose expertise, hard work, and commitment to the project brought the publication of the text to fruition. Additionally, we thank Deborah Kennedy, who provided valuable feedback on the chapters as well as a careful copy edit. We also acknowledge the efforts of Emily Christenson of Paintbox Creative, who is responsible for the page layout and cover design.

The development of a text is a complex, albeit exciting, process. We owe a debt of gratitude to Kate Paesani, Director of the Center for Advanced Research on Language Acquisition (CARLA), who wrote the Introduction to this volume. Additionally, we are deeply grateful to our reviewers, who offered helpful comments and suggestions as well as words of encouragement throughout our writing and revision:

Lorraine Denman — University of Pittsburgh, Pittsburgh, PA
Mandy R. Menke — University of Minnesota, Minneapolis, MN
Francis J. Troyan — The Ohio State University, Columbus, OH

On a more personal note, Eileen Glisan thanks her family for their ongoing support of her professional work. Her granddaughter, Allie Andreya, continues to be a source of inspiration and energy in her life. Additionally, she dedicates this volume to the memory of Dr. Raldo Parascenzo, Professor of Spanish at California University of Pennsylvania, who was Eileen's mentor during her undergraduate years and beyond and served as a role model of a professional who devoted his life to preparing and supporting generations of language teachers.

Richard Donato thanks his daughter Claire for her constant encouragement during the writing of this volume and interest in this work. Additionally, he thanks and recognizes the contributions of his students, teaching assistants in the Department of French and Italian and the Department of Hispanic Languages and Literatures at the University of Pittsburgh, who read and reacted to early drafts of chapters and provided valuable feedback that led to strengthening and improving the volume's clarity and contents. Finally, he wishes to thank Prof. James Lantolf, Professor Emeritus at the Pennsylvania State University. His positive reaction to the first volume and his inclusion of high-leverage practices as the organizing framework in the Center for Advanced Language Proficiency Education and Research were testimony to the value and importance of this work.

We dedicate this second volume to the teacher candidates, novice and experienced teachers, and teacher educators in the field of language teaching who we hope will use this text as a mediational tool throughout their journeys as they endeavor to engage and excite language learners in their classrooms. We hope that this text unpacks the complexity of these important practices for teacher preparation and professional development programs and that it prompts ongoing conversation regarding the teaching practices that have the power to leverage language learning and development in exciting ways.

TABLE OF CONTENTS

INTRODUCTION

When I wrote the introduction to the first volume of *Enacting the Work of Language Instruction: High-Leverage Teaching Practices* in 2016, I had just taught a methods course for K-16 teachers of various languages for the first time in over a decade. In preparing that course, the concept of praxis—or the dialogic relationship between what teachers know (i.e., research-based principles) and what they are able to do (i.e., classroom practice)—was foundational to my thinking (Lantolf & Poehner, 2014). Since then, praxis has come to define much of what I do as a teacher-scholar: It is reflected in the projects, resources, and professional development carried out at the Center for Advanced Research on Language Acquisition (CARLA); it undergirds my research into teacher understandings and implementation of multiliteracies pedagogy; and it frames the courses I teach, both those for undergraduate students of French and those for graduate student teacher-learners.

In 2018, I had the opportunity to teach methods again, this time for new graduate students in French, German, and Spanish at the University of Minnesota. The course provided these teacher-learners with their first look into the science of teaching and how it is manifested in lower-level postsecondary language classrooms. Praxis therefore played an essential role in the design and implementation of this methods course, as well. Indeed, the high-leverage teaching practices (HLTPs) introduced in Volume I of *Enacting the Work of Language Instruction* provided praxis-based grounding for the research studied in the course. Specifically, students read about these practices in relation to key pedagogical and theoretical concepts from communicative and multiliteracies approaches (Paesani, Allen, & Dupuy, 2016; Shrum & Glisan, 2016); deconstructed each practice; brainstormed ways to apply practices in their classrooms; and reported back to the class. This enactment sequence, which was mediated by methods course activities, tools presented in the readings, and follow-up discussions, demonstrates the flexibility of the cycle suggested in both volumes of *Enacting the Work of Language Instruction*, which can be adapted to fit the affordances and constraints of various teacher education contexts.

Given the integration of HLTPs into the methods course, I was thrilled when the authors invited me to write this introduction to Volume II of *Enacting the Work of Language Instruction*. I was eager to discover the new practices and to consider how they might fit into the next iteration of the methods course. As I began reading the manuscript, it was immediately evident how these four practices could be used to support additional theoretical and pedagogical concepts introduced in the methods course, including backward design, student learning outcomes, and genre-based writing instruction. Also striking was the interconnectedness of the HLTPs introduced in both books: The study and enactment of one practice, such as *establishing a meaningful and purposeful context for language instruction* (HLTP #7, Volume II), supports the study and enactment of another, such as *facilitating target language comprehensibility* (HLTP #1, Volume I). Finally, because each of these practices is centered on those "tasks and activities that are essential for skillful beginning teachers to understand, take responsibility for, and be prepared to carry out in order to enact their core instructional responsibilities" (Ball & Forzani, 2009, p. 504), rather than on a specific method or approach, HLTPs from Volumes I and II complement the communicative- and multiliteracies-oriented curriculum of my methods course. Indeed, this is the beauty of the HLTPs presented in *Enacting the Work of Language Instruction*: They can be mixed, matched, and introduced in any order that makes sense for teacher education programs, regardless of its pedagogical or theoretical orientation.

Volume II of *Enacting the Work of Language Instruction* fills an important void in HLTP scholarship by introducing four additional core practices, grounded in current research on second language acquisition, language pedagogy, and teacher development. Yet since the publication of Volume I, surprisingly little research investigating HLTPs in K-12 and postsecondary language learning contexts has been published, despite multiple calls for this work (e.g., Davin & Troyan, 2015; Hlas & Hlas, 2012; Kearney, 2015; Paesani, Allen, Donato, & Kearney, 2017). Research emerging over the past four years has focused on defining language-specific HLTPs (e.g., Goldman, 2019; Neri, Lozano, Chang, & Herman, 2017; Zhai, 2019) and on preparing language teachers to use HLTPs (e.g. Peercy, Varghese, & Dubetz, 2019; Troyan & Peercy, 2016). The current book, which provides a more robust set of teaching practices, creates an opportunity for increased and innovative research into HLTPs in language education. Investigating how these practices are enacted in K-12 and postsecondary classrooms will help us better understand teacher practice and its impact on student learning, and will help determine the sub-practices that are most salient for each HLTP. In addition, studying how educators mediate teachers' understanding and enactment of HLTPs will contribute to current research on teacher conceptual development, in general, and on responsive mediation, in particular (e.g., Johnson & Golombek, 2016, 2020). Longitudinal research on HLTP enactment and mediation is also needed, not only for deeper understandings of teacher learning, but also for the creation of additional tools and resources to support teachers and teacher educators in implementing and refining practices essential to carrying out praxis-based language instruction. An example is the podcast series, presented in the form of TedEd lessons, created by the National Foreign Language Resource Center (NFLRC) at the University of Hawai'i. This tool enhances the chapters in *Enacting the Work of Language Instruction* by providing insights into and additional resources for each HLTP presented in Volume I (NFLRC, 2019).

An important focus of the body of work on HLTPs has been on novice teachers and what they need to know and be able to do to teach successfully in K-12 and postsecondary language classrooms. Yet in this book's preliminary chapter, the authors are careful to emphasize that the HLTPs they introduce represent the minimum expectations for both novice and experienced language teachers. Moving forward, it will be important to consider this latter group more deliberately. Not only is there much to learn from their classroom experiences, but experienced teachers also require continued support as they hone their practices and deepen their conceptual understandings. Moreover, in postsecondary language departments, as well as in Advanced Placement and International Baccalaureate programs at the secondary level, these more experienced instructors are often teaching courses grounded in literary-cultural content. Understanding which HLTPs are relevant for such courses and how those HLTPs are applied in them will be key to supporting this group of teachers. For instance, in an advanced methods course focused on how best to teach literary-cultural content, teacher-learners might explore in greater depth HLTP #3, *guiding learners to interpret and discuss authentic texts* (Volume I) and HLTP #9, *engaging learners in purposeful written communication* (Volume II). In studying practices and pedagogies that prioritize critical engagement with target language texts and development of advanced language functions such as communicating in paragraph-length discourse across time frames (ACTFL, 2012), these two HLTPs can be put into dialogue with one another in ways that go beyond the minimum expectations for effective language teaching.

Attention to experienced teachers also provides opportunities to more fully understand and encourage teachers' adaptive expertise as it develops over time. In Chapter 5 below the authors define 'adaptive expertise' as "the ability to modify and extend the instructional moves previously deconstructed in order to address novel instructional situations and learner needs." Longitudinal observation of how more experienced teachers (i.e., those who have likely internalized the routines associated with a given HLTP) exercise the decision making, agency, creativity, and experimentation needed to modify HLTPs for use in a range of contexts can inform the ways we might support less experienced teachers in becoming adaptive experts. Furthermore, providing novice and experienced instructors with praxis-based resources, tools, and professional development experiences that support specific HLTPs creates an optimal environment for fostering adaptive expertise. CARLA's Summer Institute Program provides an interesting testing ground for cultivating this expertise. Our audience is comprised of novice and experienced instructors who are eager to fine-tune their current practices and appropriate new knowledge and techniques. In my own summer institute on foreign language literacies development, for instance, teachers represent contexts ranging from middle school English as a second language (ESL) to post-secondary Chinese culture, and experience levels ranging from one to over 20 years in the classroom. An important objective of this institute is to create literacies-oriented lessons that foster deep engagement with target language texts and reflect theoretical and pedagogical concepts explored through readings and class discussions. The tools presented in Chapter 1 for *establishing a meaningful and purposeful context for language instruction* will help teachers meet this learning objective, develop routine expertise, and adapt what they have learned for their specific context and learner needs. I am thus eager to experiment with this and other HLTPs from Volume II of *Enacting the Work of Language Instruction* in my summer institute and beyond to foster teachers' agency and creativity and support them as they develop students' interpersonal, interpretive, and presentational communication through engagement with target language texts.

Kate Paesani
Director, Center for Advanced Research on Language Acquisition (CARLA)
University of Minnesota

References

ACTFL. (2012). *ACTFL proficiency guidelines 2012.* Alexandria, VA: Author.

Ball, D. L., & Forzani, F. M. (2009). The work of teaching and the challenge of teacher education. *Journal of Teacher Education,* 60, 497-511.

Davin, K. J., & Troyan, F. J. (2015). The implementation of high-leverage teaching practices: From the university classroom to the field site. *Foreign Language Annals, 48*, 124-142.

Goldman, J. (2019). Six high-leverage writing practices for teaching English language learners in English language arts. In L. de Oliveira, K. Obenchain, R. Kenney, & A. Oliveira (Eds.), *Teaching the content areas to English language learners in secondary schools. English language education, Volume 17* (pp. 65-84). Basel, Switzerland: Springer.

Hlas, A. C., & Hlas, C. S. (2012). A review of high-leverage teaching practices: Making connections between mathematics and foreign languages. *Foreign Language Annals, 45*(S1), S76-S97.

Johnson, K. E., & Golombek, P. R. (2016). *Mindful L2 teacher education: A sociocultural perspective on cultivating teachers' professional development*. New York: Routledge.

Johnson, K. E., & Golombek, P. R. (2020). Informing and transforming language teacher education pedagogy. *Language Teaching Research, 24*, 116-127.

Kearney, E. (2015). A high-leverage language teaching practice: Leading an open-ended group discussion. *Foreign Language Annals, 48*, 100-123.

Lantolf, J. P., & Poehner, M. E. (2014). *Sociocultural theory and the pedagogical imperative in L2 education: Vygotskian praxis and the research/practice divide*. New York: Routledge.

Neri, R., Lozano, M., Chang, S., & Herman, J. (2017). *High-leverage principles of effective instruction for English learners. From college and career ready standards to teaching and learning in the classroom: A series of resources for teachers.* Los Angeles: The Regents of the University of California.

NFLRC. (2019). *High-leverage teaching practices*. Retrieved from https://nflrc.hawaii.edu/events/view/120/

Paesani, K., Allen, H. W., Donato, R., & Kearney, E. (2017, February). Perspectives on high-leverage teaching practices. Panel presentation at the 10th International Conference on Language Teacher Education, University of California, Los Angeles.

Paesani, K., Allen, H. W., & Dupuy, B. (2016). *A multiliteracies framework for collegiate foreign language teaching*. Upper Saddle River, NJ: Pearson.

Peercy, M. M., Varghese, M., & Dubetz, N. (2019). Critically examining practice-based teacher education for teachers of language minoritized youth. *TESOL Quarterly, 53*, 1173-1185.

Shrum, J. L., & Glisan, E. W. (2016). *Teacher's handbook: Contextualized language instruction* (5th ed.). Boston: Cengage.

Troyan, F. J., & Peercy, M. M. (2016). Novice teachers' perspectives on learning in lesson rehearsals in second language teacher preparation. *International Multilingual Research Journal, 10*(3), 188-200.

Zhai, L. (2019). Illuminating the enactment of high-leverage teaching practices in an exemplary world language teaching video library. *American Educational Research Journal, 56*(5), 1681–1717. https://doi.org/10.3102/0002831218824289

Preliminary Chapter

Completing the Set of High-Leverage Teaching Practices for Language Instruction

The field of teacher education is currently in the midst of an evolution that situates *practice* at the center of teacher education with a focus on preparing teachers to enact the work of teaching. In fact, in recent years, the notion of engaging prospective teachers in *doing* teaching rather than simply *talking about* it has begun to take root, largely as a result of research and professional dialogue in the area of high-leverage teaching practices (HLTPs) (Hlas & Hlas, 2012; Sleep, 2009). HLTPs are the "tasks and activities that are essential for skillful beginning teachers to understand, take responsibility for, and be prepared to carry out in order to enact their core instructional responsibilities" (Ball & Forzani, 2009, p. 504). Professional discussion has centered on the identification of specific high-leverage teaching practices, often called *core practices*, across disciplines and levels of instruction that are essential for novices to control "before they are permitted to assume independent responsibility for a classroom" (Forzani, 2014, p. 357). Although the concept of HLTP is directed specifically to what is necessary to become an accomplished novice teacher, these practices have also been found to be critical to the work of *all* teachers and therefore not exclusively relevant to only those newly initiated into the profession (Zhai, 2019).

The first volume of *Enacting the Work of Language Instruction: High-Leverage Teaching Practices* introduced foreign language educators to the concept of HLTPs and presented a set of six practices that are essential for teachers, both novice and experienced, to enact in their classrooms to support second language learning and development. The book was designed to assist language teachers in enacting these six practices by deconstructing and practicing them within a broader 'Cycle of Enactment' that also features rehearsal, coaching, and self-assessment (Grossman & McDonald, 2008; Lampert et al., 2013; Lampert & Graziani, 2009). Presented in the first volume were the following six HLTPs, selected because "they are learnable in initial teacher preparation programs, have been shown to be developmentally appropriate for novices, represent fundamental skills of language teaching, are interconnected and mutually support each other (i.e., one builds on the other), and are key to supporting students' language learning" (Glisan & Donato, 2017, p. 11):

HLTP#1: Facilitating Target Language Comprehensibility

HLTP#2: Building a Classroom Discourse Community

HLTP#3: Guiding Learners to Interpret and Discuss Authentic Texts

HLTP#4: Focusing on Form in a Dialogic Context Through PACE

HLTP#5: Focusing on Cultural Products, Practices, and Perspectives in a Dialogic Context

HLTP#6: Providing Oral Corrective Feedback to Improve Learner Performance

It is important to note four caveats regarding these six HLTPs. First, these practices are *complex* inasmuch as they consist of a set of 'instructional moves' that are not always visible to an observer (Ball & Forzani, 2009; Lewis, 2007). Thus, modeling alone is insufficient for teaching a novice how to carry out these fundamental practices of language instruction. Second, they are necessary for teachers to engage in 'ambitious teaching'—that is, "instructional experiences that support students in carrying out cognitively demanding tasks" (Troyan, Davin, & Donato, 2013, p. 174). Third, these six HLTPs represent *minimum* expectations for both novices and more experienced teachers alike and therefore do not represent the maximum scope of what a language teacher should be able to do in the classroom. Finally, as stated in the first volume, "these practices are not the only HLTPs that ...teachers should know, and there are others" (Glisan & Donato, 2017, p. 11; see also Zhai, 2009).

This second volume continues the discussion of HLTPs as they apply to the field of foreign language instruction and presents four additional practices that all language teachers should be able to perform in the classroom. The inclusion of these practices in this volume completes the set of 10 HLTPs that language teachers should be expected to enact, as a minimum, in their classrooms in order to bring about language development and learning on the part of their learners. These four practices, which will be explained, deconstructed, and detailed, form the focus of this volume:

HLTP#7: Establishing a Meaningful and Purposeful Context for Language Instruction

HLTP#8: Planning for Instruction Using an Iterative Process for Backward Design

HLTP#9: Engaging Learners in Purposeful Written Communication

HLTP#10: Developing Contextualized Performance Assessments

Rationale for Inclusion of the Final Four HLTPs

The first set of six practices addressed how to make target language use comprehensible; how to build a classroom discourse community; how to guide learners to interpret and discuss authentic texts; how to focus on form as well as on cultural products, practices, and perspectives in a dialogic context; and how to provide oral corrective feedback. These HLTPs feature a primary focus on oral interpersonal communication, which is undeniably paramount in the language classroom. However, there are four additional practices that teachers should be able to enact as a minimum in order to address the fuller picture of language learning and classroom practice while providing further support for oral and written communication. As was the case with the six HLTPs introduced in the first volume, these four practices should be familiar to a language professional as part of a teacher preparation program. Consequently, teachers should recognize their usefulness for teaching and facilitating language learning. While these four practices are equally challenging, they do, however, share two characteristics that set them apart from the initial six HLTPs:

1. The theoretical basis for these practices emanated from more general educational theory, research, and practice dealing with issues in learning and development. That is, this research was done outside of foreign language education or second language acquisition and then applied to our field. Thus, enactment of these practices involves an understanding of specialized knowledge from the wider educational arena and how to apply that knowledge to language teaching.

2. Although these practices have a theoretical basis, they have been less clearly developed in the literature on language teaching because they are more complex and not as widely researched. Hence, the pedagogical moves involved in them are less visible and more complex than was the case with the first six HLTPs, but equally essential for teachers to engage in ambitious teaching as defined earlier. Additionally, because some practices represent a subcategory of a larger grain-size practice (e.g., backward planning as one effective approach in the general practice of instructional planning), the research base may not be as extensive as it is on, for example, the focusing of target language form in a dialogic context or providing oral corrective feedback (see HLTP Volume I).

Each of the four additional practices is introduced below with a brief rationale for why it is important as a minimal expectation for all language teachers.

HLTP #7: Establishing a Meaningful and Purposeful Context for Language Instruction

A look back at the evolution of language teaching can serve as a reminder that for many decades, language classrooms consisted of meaningless repetition and recitation of dialogues that had little connection to conversations that one might actually hear in the world beyond the classroom. That is, a stumbling block in the language teaching of yesteryear was the virtual absence of meaning—i.e., a 'meaningful context' in the activities and exchanges that students were expected to carry out. While a fuller discussion of 'context' will occur in the chapter that presents this practice, it is important here to consider that context includes "the setting, topic, situation, purpose, actors, roles, cultural assumptions, goals, and motivation that are involved in the communication" (Shrum & Glisan, 2015, p. 44). The issue of context is critical to motivating learners to see the value and importance of learning another language, to establishing clearly defined reasons and purposes for communication in cultural contexts, and to facilitating the learning process. Further, establishing a meaningful context is paramount for a language teacher to have success in enacting the six practices featured in the earlier HLTP volume and the practices that are presented in this one. In fact, the importance of context is mentioned in each of the six HLTPs deconstructed in the first volume, which lends additional support to its inclusion here as its own practice.

It may seem to some that the first practice a novice teacher must learn to enact is to design a lesson plan. However, in order to design a plan, one must first establish a meaningful context for the plan. Establishing a context presents a challenge for language teachers, in particular for novice teachers, as this practice prompts questions such as: How do I go about selecting a context? On what basis do I determine that a context is appropriate and will be effective in providing a framework for meaningful language use? And perhaps more importantly, how do I use the context to 'drive' my unit and daily lessons so that meaning remains at the forefront? In this regard, it is not uncommon in language textbooks to find a superficial theme (e.g., the city, school life, holidays) presented as context at the start of a lesson/chapter but often not carried through the subsequent activities—that is, the context seems to disappear as the focus of the chapter defaults to grammar and vocabulary devoid of meaning and purposeful communication. One tool for assisting teachers in maintaining the focus on context throughout a unit of instruction is the identification of an 'inquiry question,' which is an overarching inquiry in the form of a question to investigate or a problem to solve. This will be explored later as part of the high-leverage practice of establishing a meaningful context for teaching.

HLTP #8: Planning for Instruction Using an Iterative Process for Backward Design

Few would argue with the claim that teachers should be able to design instructional plans, be they unit plans or daily lesson plans. Effective planning undergirds all of the HLTPs presented for language teachers, yet this practice is often elusive, especially for novice teachers, who may be tempted to follow a textbook in page-by-page fashion based on the belief that the 'plan' has already been laid out for them in the chapter. The problem with relying too heavily on the textbook is that classroom activities are often strung together with little or no attention to what learners will be expected to know or be able do by the end of the unit, chapter, or lesson. Lesson planning presents a challenge given that there are many moving parts and factors to consider; in the absence of guidelines on how to deconstruct this practice, it can indeed become overwhelming. Additionally, planning a sequence of instruction in units, chapters, and lessons requires the ability to build coherence across tasks in ways that result in student success rather than student confusion or frustration.

The typical approach taken to this HLTP is to present a backward-design process for planning, one that begins with a focus on the desired end results of a unit or lesson (Wiggins & McTighe, 2005). However, the approach presented here goes further in illustrating the stages as being *iterative*—that is, work on one phase of the backward planning process may necessitate a return to a previous phase to make changes in the plan. Just as establishing a meaningful context is necessary for maintaining purposeful language use, keeping end results at the forefront in planning is critical in enabling learners to reach targeted outcomes or goals. Teachers learn to enact this practice by identifying desired end results and assessment evidence *before* creating the learning experiences and instructional tasks and activities that they will use to help students achieve the desired results. This HLTP engages teachers in using the context and inquiry question presented through implementation of HLTP #7 as the foundation for establishing end results, assessment evidence, and the learning plan—thus connecting these two practices in a seamless fashion.

HLTP #9: Engaging Learners in Purposeful Written Communication

An important outcome of language teaching is to enable students to present information, concepts, and ideas on a variety of topics and in various forms of written texts. This HLTP concerns how teachers can support the development of students' ability to create written texts as described in the presentational communication standard of the Communication Goal Area in the *World-Readiness Standards for Learning Languages* (The National Standards Collaborative Board, 2015). With a few notable exceptions (Abdel-Malek, 2019; Byrnes, 2009; Troyan, 2014; Yasuda, 2011), a pedagogy for developing written presentational communication is not as well developed in the field of foreign language education as it is in the extensive research base and pedagogical recommendations that exist for teaching English as a second language (see for example Storch, 2013; Swales, 2004; and the *Journal of Second Language Writing*, 1992-present). Additionally, writing in a language class is often reduced to the transcription of the students' spoken language rather than the conscious application of discourse moves that shape the specific ways that a particular piece of writing is constructed for its intended purpose, readership, and cultural context. For this HLTP, we draw on recent work on genre-based pedagogy inspired by the Sydney School and informed by Systemic Functional Linguistics for designing writing instruction across a variety of genres. In this model of instruction, 'genre' is to be understood as texts written (or spoken) for specific *purposes* in sociocultural contexts. Genre is not to be confused with its meaning in the context of the literary arts (prose, poetry, drama, etc.). Although the number of sociocultural purposes for which texts can be written is extensive, Derewianka (2009) provides a few common genres that seem to appear across cultures: recounts, instructions, narratives, informational reports, explanations, and arguments.

The genre-based approach to writing maintains that text structure for specific genres, such as those listed above, needs to be made visible to students and that the discourse moves for particular texts can often be represented as conventionalized and probabilistic discourse practices. What this means for pedagogy is that teachers need to make students aware of how texts work (Derewianka, 2009) by analyzing models of texts and identifying how particular genres are constructed and unfold in written form. The genre-based approach to writing that is introduced in this volume is based on Troyan's recommendations and the work of Derewianka. This HLTP engages teachers in deconstructing how this approach may be carried out across all levels of FL instruction, thus supporting students' proficiency in composing written texts of various kinds.

HLTP #10: Developing Contextualized Performance Assessments

Over the past several decades, assessment in foreign language education has evolved so that it is no longer viewed as a separate component that a teacher conceptualizes *after* instruction has occurred and for the purpose of assigning grades to students. Instead, the current view of assessment is that it forms a seamless connection with instruction and should be addressed *before* and *during* instruction so that there is evidence of student progress in meeting desired results while instruction is under way. In view of this critical link between instruction and assessment, knowing how to design a language assessment is a high-leverage practice.

While there are myriad types of assessments that teachers can develop for formative and summative purposes, this HLTP is presented in terms of three smaller-grain practices that should be a minimum expectation of all language teachers, be they novices or more experienced:

- Creating and administering oral interpersonal performance assessments;
- Creating presentational writing assessments; and
- Providing feedback to learners through performance assessment rubrics.

This HLTP is a logical extension of the other high-leverage practices for assessing learner performance in terms of reflecting both the desired end results identified in the iterative process for backward design and the meaningful context and inquiry question that frames the unit of instruction. In considering this HLTP, teachers will learn how to design an oral interpersonal assessment and will explore ways in which oral assessment can be conducted within the classroom setting. In addition, they will enact the practice of creating a presentational genre-based writing assessment that engages learners in writing purposefully to achieve goals in social and cultural contexts. Finally, they will explore ways to provide feedback to learners by developing and using performance assessment rubrics. Knowing how to enact these three basic assessment practices can be the foundation for enacting more complex assessment practices such as the Integrated Performance Assessment (IPA) and Dynamic Assessment (DA) as the teacher gains more experience in the classroom.

Organization of Volume II

The organization of the second volume mirrors the organization of the first one. Specifically, each of the following four chapters presents one HLTP; in some cases, a large-grain-size practice is broken into a few smaller-grain-size practices to be deconstructed. Throughout all chapters, each key term that is used for the first time appears in **boldface** along with its definition. Readers should remember important terms in the text, some of which may be cross-referenced with a methods book for further explanation and elaboration.
The four chapters are organized in the following manner:

Research and Theory Supporting the Practice: Each chapter begins with a justification for selection of the practice as high-leverage and situates it within research and theory. As this section is only a thumbnail overview, only the most relevant research findings and theoretical frameworks are presented. The reader is encouraged to read more in-depth treatments of this research by consulting *Teacher's Handbook: Contextualized Language Instruction*, 5th edition (Shrum & Glisan, 2016). References for all cited resources appear at the end of each chapter.

Considerations about the Practice: This section features an explication of the key points, including caveats regarding the practice, discussed from the standpoint of a series of questions that novice and at times experienced teachers typically ask. Readers will find that this part is constructed as if it were an informal dialogue with the teacher.

Deconstructing the Practice: Next, the practice is 'deconstructed' into a series of detailed steps that the teacher can follow in rehearsal, practice, and enactment. It should be noted that this careful deconstruction is the hallmark of an HLTP and until now has not been done in foreign language education, and that the steps suggested must be carried out while simultaneously keeping in mind the unique instructional context of each teacher, including the level of the learners, the lesson goals, how learners are motivated, and other factors.

To this end, there is always flexibility with the specific steps, content, and level of challenge of each practice. In this way, the practices can be adapted to address the realities of each teacher's instructional context. Therefore, we opted not to include entire sample lessons that illustrate each HLTP so as not to create the misunderstanding that there is only one way for each practice to be enacted within lessons. Teachers may also find it helpful to consult the rubrics that accompany each HLTP as they deconstruct the practice.

Rehearsing the Practice: This section enables teachers to put into practice and rehearse the deconstructed steps that they have just learned. These activities are designed for pre-service teachers enrolled in methods courses and/or clinical experiences, teaching assistants at the university level, and in-service K-12 teachers. In this regard, the tasks can be done in collaboration with classmates, in the case of pre-service teachers, or colleagues, in the case of in-service teachers. Some chapters feature multiple activities that are sequenced to enable teachers to focus on specific aspects of the practice before rehearsing the whole practice (referred to as 'approximations of practice'). It should be noted that answers are not provided for these activities because they are designed to prompt reflection, analysis, and discussion, and because specific responses do not necessarily apply to all instructional contexts. It is important to note that the rehearsal of an HLTP must be placed in some instructional activity with a clear purpose and goal (Teaching Works, 2020). HLTPs cannot be rehearsed and practiced in a void and are always used in the service of some larger instructional goal. Teachers will find it helpful to consult the 'External Mediational Tools' (EMTs) (see explanation under 'Features Maintained from Volume I' below) and rubrics that accompany each HLTP before beginning the rehearsal stage.

Assessing the Practice: Teachers may use the rubrics that accompany each HLTP in self-assessing their own performance and/or to assist a peer or colleague in assessing performance. It should be noted that 'rubrics' are a tool for assessing performance based on specific criteria and detailed performance descriptions for each point or level of performance (Wiggins & McTighe, 2005). As in the first volume, the rubrics developed for the HLTPs in this text have the following characteristics:

- They describe the criteria by which teachers' enactment of the practices can be assessed; e.g., these three to five criteria address the instructional moves that were deconstructed and rehearsed within each chapter; and
- They use a range of four performance levels to rate teachers' performance according to the degree to which the criteria have been met:
    - Exceeds Expectations
    - Meets Expectations—High
    - Meets Expectations—Low
    - Does Not Meet Expectations.
- It should be noted that the 'Exceeds Expectations' category describes performance that is far beyond what most novice teachers are able to do, and thus only a small percentage of teachers are likely to demonstrate performance at this level. Nonetheless, as is the case with all useful rubrics, the HLTP rubrics include this level of

performance to define how teachers may go beyond the minimal expectations and to encourage a higher level of performance.

The HLTP rubrics serve three purposes:

1. To define expectations for enacting the practices before teachers rehearse them—that is, to describe what effective performance looks like even before the practices are enacted;

2. To assist teachers in self-assessing how they enact the practice and identifying specific areas of the practice that may need attention;

3. To rate teachers' performance and provide feedback so that they can reflect on and improve their ability to enact the practices.

A set of rubrics for each HLTP appears at the end of the chapter and can be easily duplicated for use. For information regarding how to assign grades or scores based on performance ratings using a rubric, see Shrum and Glisan 2016, pp. 384-387.

Putting the Practice into a Larger Context: Addressing Instructional Goals and Challenges: Each of the four chapters concludes by prompting teachers to think about the practice within the larger context of their teaching and as an avenue for addressing common teaching challenges that they confront in today's classrooms. Thus, the teaching practice is placed into the wider context of educational issues and priorities and teachers' classroom experiences. Further, this discussion provides additional support to help novice teachers understand the HLTPs through the lens of 'decision-making' practices and *not* 'imitative practices' followed in a prescriptive procedural manner (Kennedy, 2016).

A New Feature of the Text: From Deconstruction to Enactment and Adaptation

In the first volume, the final chapter presented the Cycle of Enactment model to illustrate how teachers might learn to enact the HLTPs, how they might collaborate with others as they engage in enacting the practices, and how they might reflect on and assess/self-assess their progress along the way. In Volume II, we end with a detailed treatment of how teachers can move from deconstructing the practices to enacting them, and ultimately to using greater creativity in adapting the practices. Novice teachers can develop skill in enacting HLTPs in a routinized manner while also expanding their teaching repertoire by adapting certain aspects of these practices to fit their instructional contexts and the needs of their learners. The final chapter addresses several factors that are instrumental in prompting teachers to embrace and reconstruct HLTPs: situating HLTPs within instructional activities; the teacher's will or motivation for embracing the HLTPs; and the role of decision making, dialogic mediation, and coaching in developing adaptive expertise. Suggestions are offered for how teachers can recompose the deconstructed practices, whether they are at the novice or more experienced ends of the teaching continuum.

Features of the Text Maintained from Volume I

In addition to a helpful list of references and rubrics for each HLTP, the end of each chapter features External Mediational Tools (EMTs) to assist teachers in enacting the practices. These EMTs are resources that list the key instructional moves for each HLTP (i.e., a 'cheat sheet' of sorts), many of which appear in the form of checklists and may be photocopied for use by the teacher.

Finally, another feature of this text is that it can be used to assist college faculty as they prepare their teacher preparation programs to undergo national recognition review by ACTFL and the Council for Accreditation of Educator Preparation (CAEP), the agency that accredits colleges and universities and "recognizes" their teacher preparation programs. To this end, each HLTP is cross-referenced with the pertinent ACTFL/CAEP Program Standards for the Preparation of Foreign Language Teachers (ACTFL, 2013) to assist faculty in collecting evidence needed for an ACTFL/CAEP national recognition program review. Teacher preparation faculty will find this cross reference helpful inasmuch as the standards represent national expectations for what beginning language teachers should know and be able to do in the classroom. A summary of the standards appears in Appendix A, and the full description of the standards can be found at https://bit.ly/3fJmIJc.

References

Abdel-Malek, M. (2019). Writing recounts of habitual events: Investigating a genre-based approach. *Foreign Language Annals, 52*(2), 373-387.

American Council on the Teaching of Foreign Languages (2013). *ACTFL/CAEP program standards for the preparation of foreign language teachers.* Alexandria, VA: Author. Retrieved from https://bit.ly/3fJmIJc

Ball, D. L., & Forzani, F. M. (2009). The work of teaching and the challenge for teacher education. *Journal of Teacher Education, 60*(5), 497-511.

Byrnes, H. (2009). Emergent L2 German writing ability in a curricular context: A longitudinal study of grammatical metaphor. *Linguistics and Education, 20*(1)B, 50-66.

Derewianka, B. (2009). *Exploring how texts work.* Laura Street Newton NSW: Primary Teaching Association (Australia).

Forzani, F. M. (2014). Understanding "core practices" and "practice-based" teacher education: Learning from the past. *Journal of Teacher Education, 65*(4), 357-368.

Glisan, E. W., & Donato, R. (2017). *Enacting the work of language instruction: High-leverage teaching practices.* Alexandria, VA: ACTFL.

Grossman, P., & McDonald, M. (2008). Back to the future: Directions for research in teaching and teacher education. *American Educational Research Journal, 45*(1), 184-205.

Hlas, A. C., & Hlas, C. S. (2012). A review of high-leverage teaching practices: Making connections between mathematics and foreign languages. *Foreign Language Annals, 45,* s76-s97.

Kennedy, M. (2016). Parsing the practice of teaching. *Journal of Teacher Education, 67*(1), 6-17.

Lampert, M., Franke, M., Kazemi, E., Ghousseini, H., Turrou, A., Beasley, H., & Crowe, K. (2013). Keeping it complex: Using rehearsals to support novice teacher learning of ambitious teaching. *Journal of Teacher Education, 64,* 226-243.

Lampert, M., & Graziani, F. (2009). Instructional activities as a tool for teachers' and teacher educators' learning in and for practice. *Elementary School Journal, 109*, 491–509.

Lewis, J. M. (2007). *Teaching as invisible work.* Unpublished dissertation. University of Michigan, Ann Arbor.

Shrum, J. L., & Glisan, E. W. (2016). *Teacher's handbook: Contextualized language instruction* (5th ed.). Boston: Cengage Learning.

Sleep, L. (2009). *Teaching to the mathematical point: Knowing and using mathematics in teaching.* Unpublished doctoral dissertation. University of Michigan, Ann Arbor.

Storch, N. (2013). *Collaborative writing in L2 classrooms.* Bristol, UK: Multilingual Matters.

Swales, J. M. (2004). *Research genre: Exploration and applications.* Cambridge, MA: Cambridge University Press.

Teaching Works. (2020). *High-leverage practices.* Retrieved from http://www.teachingworks.org/work-of-teaching/high-leverage-practices

The National Standards Collaborative Board. (2015). *World-readiness standards for learning languages.* Alexandria, VA: Author.

Troyan, F. J. (2014). Leveraging genre theory: A genre-based interactive model for the era of the Common Core State Standards. *Foreign Language Annals, 47,* 5–24.

Troyan, F. J., Davin, K. J., & Donato, R. (2013). Exploring a practice-based approach to foreign language teacher preparation: A work in progress. *Canadian Modern Language Review/La revue canadienne des langues vivantes, 69,* 154-180.

Wiggins, G., & McTighe, J. (2005). *Understanding by design.* Alexandria, VA: ASCD.

Yasuda, S. (2011). Genre-based tasks in foreign language writing: Developing writers' genre awareness, linguistics knowledge, and writing competence. *Journal of Second Language Writing,* 20, 111–133.

Zhai, L. (2019). Illuminating the enactment of high-leverage teaching practices in an exemplary world language teaching video library. *American Educational Research Journal, 56*(5), 1681–1717. https://doi.org/10.3102/0002831218824289

Chapter 1

HLTP #7: Establishing a Meaningful and Purposeful Context for Language Instruction

A context is meaningful when it matters to students and involves topics and interactions to which students can relate and that they perceive as useful to their learning and future use of the target language outside of class.

All teachers, including those with even the most rudimentary knowledge of instructional practices in foreign language education, are aware that context plays an important role when planning lessons and units and carrying out instruction. The terms 'context' and 'contextualization' are pervasive in methodology textbooks devoted to preparing teachers with the theoretical foundations of instruction and the ability to plan for and enact the work of teaching. The purpose of this chapter is to look closely at what is meant by context, to describe how context can be analyzed and applied to language teaching, to deconstruct this process, and to understand why it is critically important to language instruction.

One reason context is essential to instruction is that it motivates learners by establishing clearly defined reasons and purposes for communication in cultural contexts. Context also facilitates the learning process by making meanings and language functions in speech and in written texts transparent to students. Although the concept of language function will be explored in greater detail later in the chapter, a **language function** is defined as *what* individuals *do* with language and *how* they use language to realize a goal, carry out an activity with others, meet their personal needs, or express meanings, to name only a few functional uses of language. All of the following are examples of language functions in context: ordering a meal in a restaurant or online, sending a text message to a friend to ask for directions, exchanging information in a conversation about a current event, expressing an opinion about a character in a film during a class discussion, summarizing and discussing information in an academic text. Language users carry out a multitude of language functions throughout the day to manage activities, meet needs, and get things done. The important point here is that for language instruction to be successful, it must provide frequent and sufficient opportunities for students to use language in context for various 'real life' purposes and end goals.

In addition, when information and statements are taken 'out of context' the result is often misunderstanding, confusion, or frustration. Context is therefore an overarching concept that all language teachers need to know so that they may competently plan meaningful instruction not only in terms of contextualized lessons but also across a sequence of instructional moves, materials, and assessments in a coherent fashion. Additionally, understanding the important role of context is fundamental to the successful enactment of all six practices featured in the first HLTP volume and the four practices that are presented

in this second volume. Finally, as will be seen in the next chapter, establishing a context is the first step in backward-design planning; however, it is presented here as its own HLTP due to its complexity and need to be deconstructed so that teachers are able to enact this practice successfully as the foundation on which to engage in planning.
ACTFL/CAEP Standards addressed: #3a, #4a, #4b

Research and Theory Supporting the Practice

Multiple Perspectives on Context

The concept of context has various meanings and is viewed through different perspectives in the literature. From a linguistic perspective, context often means the words surrounding an unknown word in a sentence that promote an inference about the unknown word's meaning. For example, if students already understand the meaning of the words 'mother' and 'father,' by using these context clues, they may be able to infer the meaning of the new word 'grandmother' in the sentence 'The mother of my father is my *grandmother*.' From an educational perspective, context typically refers to the specific characteristics of a classroom, school, or school system, and as such can vary from one school site to the next. From a history of language teaching perspective, context is taken to mean specific approaches and methods of instruction that have been popular over the years, such as grammar-translation, the audio-lingual method, or communicative language teaching (Shrum & Glisan, 2016). From the perspective of how the term is used in everyday conversation, context is viewed as the provision of background circumstances and situations critical for establishing mutual understandings and avoiding misunderstandings.

Before leaving this discussion of context, it is important to understand the difference between the *content* of instruction and the *context* of instruction. It is quite easy to slip into thinking that simply having content, be it situational, thematic, topical; literary, or academic, is sufficient for contextualized instruction. A useful way to understand the difference between these two terms is to consider **content** as the *what* of an act of communication (such as describing a harrowing experience or giving directions for using a new piece of technology) and **context** as the *frame* around the contents of the communication that allows the speech event to be understood properly, interpreted appropriately, and described in a relevant and accurate fashion (such as describing what is being discussed, who is talking, why they are talking, how they are talking) (Young, 2008). For example, in a reading lesson, the pre-reading task provides the context that frames the text so that the content of the reading can be understood and interpreted correctly. Without pre-reading tasks that contextualize what is read by providing background information, texts are often difficult to understand. The distinction between content and context is fundamentally important when planning for instruction. Alone, the content of a lesson, unit, interaction, or instructional task rarely leads to comprehension. Moreover, when the context is unknown, the content is often superficially understood or entirely misunderstood. For example, it is common to hear people say that they are being misinterpreted because their words were taken out of context. As Young (2008) states, the notion of context involves the juxtaposition of two entities: the speech event (what is being talked about) and a field of action (e.g., who is talking, why they are talking, how they are talking) in which the speech event is embedded.

Context and Pedagogy

From the perspective of published language learning materials or departmental curriculum guides, the term 'context' is often reduced to an overarching topic, theme or setting, such as Holidays, the City, Leisure Time Activities, At the Restaurant, Travel, or Professions, to name only a few. In this vein, some pedagogical texts suggest the integration of 'real-world contexts' that learners can connect to their own lives (Clementi & Terrill, 2013; Shrum & Glisan, 2016). Clementi and Terrill further define context through multi-dimensional global themes such as Identity, Well-Being, Belonging, Discovery, and Exploring Time and Place (2013, p. 27). Regardless of their scope, these topics, themes, and settings determine the types of vocabulary, language functions, and cultural information that students will learn, such as giving or asking for directions in the context of a city from the target language cultures, describing the jobs that various people do, or deciding on clothing for travel to international locations and climates.

There are several problems with the definitions of context summarized above and found in some published language materials. First, in some published materials, the details of the context may be shallow, uninteresting, and misleading with no compelling reasons to use the language in these pre-established settings. Second, the language used in textbook contexts may not reflect the kind of language used in communicative situations outside the classroom, thus requiring the teacher to supplement the textbook examples or correct them. In a similar vein, global themes presented in either textbooks or curriculum guides tend to be so broad that applying them to actual communicative events and language functions often proves to be challenging at best. A third consideration is that there is often no larger goal or reason beyond learning the chapter's vocabulary and grammar or completing a textbook exercise to explore the given theme or topic. For example, when students are asked to engage in a specific classroom interaction in which the theme is used as the topic of the exchange (e.g., sharing information about what foods students eat), the question still remains as to what goal and purpose drive the information exchange activity based on the theme. In the world beyond the classroom, people engage in interactions in order to gain important and useful information, create social relationships with others, or solve pressing problems. In the context of foods, for example, a larger goal beyond 'covering material' might be to exchange information with a friend about what foods to eat in order to embark on a healthier lifestyle or figure out how to follow the doctor's orders about a change of diet. In sum, a solely thematic approach presents *limitations* in terms of establishing a meaningful and purposeful context.

In a study of contextualization in several college-level textbooks, Walz (1989) shows the limitations of understanding context as only topic (health) or setting (at the doctor's office). What he observed in the textbooks that he analyzed was that thin and shallow contextualization often served only to disguise meaningless mechanical exercises and repetitive drills in which meaning took a back seat to accuracy. These ostensibly contextualized exercises were typically introduced with a brief artificial situation, e.g., *You are a doctor. Give advice to your patient on how to care for a cold. Use the imperative form of the verbs provided.* The problem here is that students may have no investment in the artificial situation because a meaningful purpose for learning this type of communicative exchange is never established. Moreover, background information is vague or lacking; for example, Who is the patient? Who is the doctor? Why is this advice important to the patient? Are there any cultural norms that need to be considered when discussing health matters? Additionally, languages offer several ways to provide advice, and using the imperative form of the verb might not always be the best option and could sound harsh and insensitive, thus misleading students on the functional uses of the imperative.

In this chapter, we maintain that to be an accomplished teacher requires a deep understanding of context and its role in language instruction. As such, context and contextualizing language teaching is a high-leverage practice essential for the competent enactment of all language lessons and units of study. Deepening understanding of the various components of context and designing meaningful cultural contexts for classroom instruction, therefore, need to be understood, planned, and integrated across all pedagogical practices. Therefore, the high-leverage practice that is introduced and deconstructed in this chapter is how to establish a meaningful and purposeful context for instruction, which ultimately is used as the overarching framework for *all* aspects of instruction, that is, for planning (e.g., long-range 'unit planning' as well as daily lesson planning), for teaching (e.g., teacher use of the target language, teacher and student interactions, and students' interactions with each other), and for assessment (e.g., formative and summative). Please note that the details of how to engage in planning within a meaningful context that has a purpose beyond learning grammar and vocabulary will be addressed in the next chapter and strategies for designing contextualized performance assessments will be discussed in a later chapter.

Research and Theory on Context

Relative to other areas of language instruction, context is one area that has not been investigated in the research literature and pedagogical practice as extensively as, for example, classroom discourse, the teaching of grammar, or the development of a specific language skill or mode of communication. As Byrnes points out, "although no one would argue with the need for contextualized foreign language instruction where students learn how to make meaning through the various forms that the target language offers, remarkably enough, we have not achieved (this type of) instructed foreign language development in a direct and principled way" (2009, p. 2). To address this critical issue in our profession, we will review some of the theoretical work that has helped us come to understand the meaning of context. From this review, a definition of context will be derived and proposed at the end of this section. For the purposes of this high-leverage practice, we define context as the hosts of factors that make language use *comprehensible, meaningful, memorable,* and *purposeful.* To this end, context provides information that has a purpose, such as "knowing how, when, and why to say what to whom" (National Standards Collaborative Board, 2015, p. 12). This definition of context goes beyond only the identification of a setting (e.g., in the city) or theme (e.g., food) and includes information on who is speaking, the interlocutors' relationship with each other, why they communicate, and the manner of communication, among other important factors presented below.

Analyzing a Context: The S-P-E-A-K-I-N-G Model

While the notion of context is pertinent when planning for instruction that includes any of the three modes of communication (interpretive, interpersonal, presentational) or any of the goal areas of the national standards (e.g., Cultures, Communities), anecdotal evidence suggests that teachers struggle the most with developing and implementing purposeful contextualized tasks for interpersonal communication, i.e., using the language in face-to-face talk and interaction. What is often observed is that speaking in language classes is often reduced to meaningless practice of language forms and vocabulary items rather than using language to accomplish a goal or solve a problem that is relevant to the students. The reason why the decontextualized practice of grammar persists may be because the concept of context as it relates to language instruction is not entirely clear or completely understood.

Dell Hymes (1972;1974) was among the first to describe the complexity of the context of a speech situation and the speaking events that take place in these speech situations. By **speaking situation**, Hymes means where and when the interaction takes place, such as at a party; by **speaking event** he means the language functions that are performed in the situation, such as casual conversation, greetings, talking about the self, complimenting, talking about likes or dislikes, or leave taking when the party has ended. When establishing contexts for instruction, both speaking situations and speaking events need to be clear in the mind of the teacher, unambiguous, and made explicit to students. The absence of this information results in what is referred to as a decontextualized lesson where students learn forms for no other reason than to display knowledge of these forms.

Using the acronym S-P-E-A-K-I-N-G, Hymes identified eight features that are necessary for understanding a communicative situation in context. To summarize briefly, the acronym S-P-E-A-K-I-N-G stands for the *setting* or scene in which the communication takes place (where and when), the *participants* involved (who), the *ends* or goals of the communication (why), and the communicative *acts*, or language functions, which are performed to meet the goals of the communication (how). To describe more completely the nature of the communicative exchange in context, Hymes includes the *key* or tone of the interaction (e.g., formal or informal, joking, serious, helpful); the *instrument* or channel through which the communication flows (e.g., e-mail messages, formal reports, webpages, face-to-face conversation); the *norms* or rules that govern the talk; and the particular cultural *genre* that shapes the communication (e.g., chit chat, academic talk, recounts, narratives, stories). In summary, the S-P-E-A-K-I-N-G model describes and determines the context by asking who the participants are, where they are, why they are communicating, and how language is being used to achieve a goal. Taken together, these features broaden the view of context in cultural settings and indicate the complex array of factors that determine who says what to whom, when, where, how and why—all critical features for creating long-lasting comprehensible meanings for participants.

Context as Field, Tenor, and Mode

A complementary perspective on describing context is found in the work of M. A. K. Halliday (2014) and involves the identification of the field, tenor, and mode of a communicative situation. Simply put, **field** refers to what is going on in the situation, that is, the topic of communication in a particular situation, the nature of the social and meaning-making activity, and the area of experience related to this activity. **Tenor** establishes who is taking part in the situation and refers to the participants, the various roles that they play, and the nature of the relationship of speakers with one another or writers with their readers. **Mode** refers to the role of language in the particular situation, the type of text produced (spoken or written), and the various ways that language brings these spoken or written texts into existence. Any change in the content of any one of these features signals a change of context.

The following example illustrates how the concepts of field, tenor, and mode have the potential to describe a context for interactions, even for those taking place in the same setting. Take, for example, a discussion about a cultural folktale with a teacher in an intermediate language class to compare or contrast it with a fairy tale from the students' culture. The field could be the level of subject matter knowledge of the students and the teacher about the genre of folktales in general, students' prior knowledge about folktales in the target language culture, their familiarity with the content of the folktale under discussion, or the students' preparation for a text-based discussion. Identification of the tenor would require examining the social rules of classroom talk and the roles the various participants play in the discussion. The teacher may be the only participant to have the status for asking questions, reducing students to the role of responders rather than initiators. Conversely, students may be observed to offer interpretations even when not asked by the teacher or to counter-question the teacher and each other when points are raised in the discussion. To identify the mode of communication would require examining how language is used to build the discussion and establish participation with the teacher and among the members of the class. Do students build a coherent discussion by responding to what was said, or are points made in a random fashion with no attention to ideas already presented about the topic of discussion? From this perspective, a classroom discussion about a cultural folktale could present quite a different context from one classroom to another. The context of the class is, therefore, described based on what is actually being discussed (e.g., factual recall vs. interpretation), how the participants interact (e.g., students only answer teacher questions or students contribute unsolicited ideas to the discussion), and how language is being used to carry out the discussion (e.g., the teacher evaluates student responses for accuracy in contrast to asking follow-up questions to encourage students to expand upon their interpretations of the folktale).

Concluding Comments on the Fundamentals of Context

The point of this brief overview of research and theory on context is to help teachers understand that context is complex and defined by a variety of situational factors—factors that are important to keep in mind when designing instruction and for connecting students to the language they are learning. Context is critical for comprehension of and meaning making in a new language, and context can never be simply reduced to the grammar point of the day (e.g., today's context is the verb 'to be'). Grammar is one tool among many that students use to make meaning, be it in terms of determining meaning from texts that they read or hear and interpret or by making themselves understood when communicating in oral or written form. While grammar is an essential tool to mediate meaning making in context, grammar is never an instructional end in and of itself and therefore cannot be the context for language instruction.

Contextualizing a series of lessons or a unit of instruction involves addressing a larger overarching question for a variety of purposes, for example, learning new information or solving an interesting problem that motivates a desire to know and captures the imagination of students. This type of inquiry, in turn, gives meaning to cultural acts of communication in speech or writing and frames classroom instruction and experiences in a way that demonstrates to students the importance and purpose of what is to be learned. Finally, the above overview of context illustrates that situations and themes alone cannot fully account for context and that in every situational context, such as a restaurant or a classroom, different kinds of speaking events could occur. Although, as presented above, the term 'context' has various meanings depending on its purpose (understanding a word in a sentence, interpreting a text, comprehending the meaning of an utterance, identifying aspects of a location), for the purpose of this high-leverage practice, **context** is understood to mean the interrelated conditions within which a communication takes place that renders the communicative event comprehensible, meaningful, appropriate, and memorable. For example, as Young (2008) states, "the place and time the interaction happened and the backgrounds of the people involved in the interaction all have an important influence on who says what to whom" (p. 15). The important point is that learning and understanding language can never be achieved in isolation and is always associated with the interrelated conditions that shape and define a context. Thus, students need to be made aware of how context in cultural settings shapes language use, how it is essential to understanding all modes of communication, and how it can support the development of language proficiency. In turn, teachers need to understand how to establish and maintain a focus on the context of an overarching unit of study (i.e., thematic unit) throughout the individual lessons that comprise the unit and assessments that are woven into instruction, in an effort to support student learning and development.

Considerations about Establishing Meaningful Contexts for Language Teaching

(1) *Each of my textbook chapters has a topic, for example, 'the city.' Why can't I just use this topic as the context for instruction?* As presented in the research and theory section of the chapter, contexts for instruction need to go beyond a simple situation or theme. At times, and in some published materials, a chapter or unit theme may relate to the vocabulary to be learned but may not identify or clarify the purpose and contextual features of instructional tasks intended to develop the modes of communication or the grammatical point introduced in the chapter. For the development of functional language proficiency, students need to be made aware not only of the overarching theme or topic that motivates interactions but also of the nature of the communicative exchanges, the persons with whom they are speaking, the goals and purposes of the interactions, cultural norms, and more. Although the topic of a chapter may be a good starting point for contextualizing a unit or lesson, the topic alone is insufficient for developing a fully contextualized lesson, establishing inquiry questions, and stating clear functional objectives that go beyond generic statements of language use (e.g., to compare, to invite, to describe). For example, the topic of 'The City' can begin the contextualization process through the use of an overarching inquiry question, such as 'How does daily life in my city compare to daily life in Madrid (or a city in another target language country)?' or 'How does the physical description of one city compare to that

of another city?' or even 'How does the physical design (description, layout) of a city affect daily life?' Investigation of any of these questions will lead to several different kinds of speaking events, such as asking a stranger on the street for directions, describing one's city to an international exchange student, stating one's likes and dislikes about one's hometown to a close friend, presenting ideas for urban planning improvement, or preparing a formal oral report that compares the plan of one's city to the plan of a city in a target language country. As illustrated in this example, the textbook topic is a good beginning, but to fully contextualize the lesson requires understanding how a well-designed question provides the overarching motivation for inquiring and communicating about the city, the kinds of communicative events that can take place in and about the city, and the contextual details of the interpersonal communication that students are learning, such as those we presented in the S-P-E-A-K-I-N-G model. In this way, students understand that they have choices when using the language and that those language choices are context-dependent and collaboratively constructed, whether in the use of formal or informal pronouns, the use of fully formed or abbreviated utterances (van Compernolle, 2015), or the use of standard language or everyday slang.

(2) *I often hear the words 'meaningful and purposeful' used with 'context.' What does this mean? What is a meaningful and purposeful context?* It is quite common to hear the phrase 'meaningful and purposeful context' for instruction, but defining this phrase can be challenging. A context is **meaningful** when it matters to students and involves topics and interactions to which students can relate and that they perceive as useful to their learning and future use of the target language outside of class. Further, the findings of research in neuroscience reveal that *meaningfulness* is pivotal in learning, given that it is the factor that has the greatest impact on whether or not information is remembered (Sousa, 2011). A context is **purposeful** when there is a real reason for student learning and a goal to achieve, not just learning for its own sake, or what Larsen-Freeman (2003) refers to as 'inert knowledge.' For a context to be purposeful, students must understand that there is a concrete outcome to their participation in the lesson that goes beyond simply 'getting the right answer,' such as coming to a group consensus about a particular topic, completing information-gap tasks of various kinds, or interpreting and deciding on the moral to a folktale.

When deciding upon meaningful and purposeful contexts for instruction, it is also important to consider the types of interactions that will take place between teacher and students and students with each other within the context of the larger area of inquiry. As presented earlier, context involves not just a situation or theme but also the nature of the communication that takes place, the participants' goals for interaction, and the participants' relationships with each other. How language is used for the purposes of learning and for achieving goals in context is equally important. As such, a context does not ensure that language will be used in ways that allow students to engage in meaning making to express their ideas, feelings, and opinions. Two examples will clarify this point. First, a teacher may select the topic 'Finding Housing' and then identify the larger area of inquiry as, 'What cultural perspectives drive the selection of housing in a particular geographical region?' Within this context, the teacher designs an oral interpersonal activity in which students play the roles of home buyer and real estate agent who discuss the features that certain homes may have according to those listed in the textbook. However, this activity can quickly become a rote exchange in which the goal becomes the use of the subjunctive with a 'model' sentence that is said repeatedly. Because the task is one that lacks relevance and meaningfulness to students and is disconnected from a larger issue to investigate, the context does not provide support for meaning making and in essence becomes a moot point.

As a second example given the topic of housing, a teacher may introduce an 'authentic text' in the context of a discussion about current housing trends, but then ask students to underline all the verbs in the text and identify their tenses. In this way, the context of the current news item introduced by the authentic text becomes only a site for mechanical practice, which, in the end, renders the context meaningless and diminishes the authenticity of the language used (see van Lier, 1996, for a discussion of authenticity and context). A way to bring greater meaning and purpose to this topic of housing could be to have students design their own lists of features they would like to have in a home they might buy or apartment they might rent. They could engage in the same student-to-student interaction described above but would be more invested in the exchange given that they would bring their own ideas and what is important to them in searching for housing. Further, students at more advanced levels might reconsider their housing preferences based on what might be available in the target culture, thus making the connection back to the inquiry question regarding cultural perspectives.

(3) *Can a grammar point be the context of instruction?* A grammar point can *never* be the context unless one is teaching a linguistics course. On the contrary, grammar itself is a tool that needs to be learned in context to enable students to comprehend the meaning and use of grammatical forms and their uses. As stated above, language, which includes the grammatical forms that are used for meaning making, can never be fully learned or understood isolated from the context in which it occurs. Simply learning verbs in the past tense for the sake of being able to conjugate past tense verbs will never reveal to students the purpose of learning the past tense or how the past tense is used for various functions in the target language. For example, observing and analyzing the use of past tense verbs by situating the learning in the context of giving a recount of one's busy day to a classmate, re-telling a folktale to a group, or reading or writing an account of an historical event in the target culture(s) are ways that raise student awareness about the meanings of past tense verbs and how the past tense is used in spoken and written texts in the target language cultural contexts.

(4) *How do I find contexts for grammar teaching when my textbook does not provide them?* A common complaint of many teachers is that the textbook includes a lot of tasks about the chapter theme or topic, but when the grammar is introduced, the theme is lost or the grammatical point is not introduced in context. Finding a context for a point of grammar is not always easy, especially when the textbook does not make the context of use clear and presents grammar as disconnected from the overall chapter topical theme. As one teacher anecdotally noted, some textbooks (not all) are simply 'grammar manuals' disguised in a superficial context. The issue is, however, that grammar should never be the point of departure for planning instruction. On the contrary,

grammar is taught and learned at the service of meaning making appropriate to the context. As will be seen in HLTP #8 in the next chapter, it is the context that determines the grammar that is necessary for achieving communicative goals; the grammatical structure does not shape the context. From this perspective, teachers consider how grammar functions in the context of everyday formal and informal activities and what *specific* grammatical elements are needed for exploring the topic or theme and for responding to the inquiry question. This process of going from the world to the lesson or unit plan is contrary to planning instruction based on exhaustive lectures on grammar rules and exceptions. For example, a context dealing with vacations, with the question of exploring how vacation preferences have changed over the years, may require the grammatical notion of habitual aspect by using the imperfect tense (what 'used to be'). In this regard, students could discuss what vacations used to be like, including how their own families spent their vacations, which would naturally require the use of the grammatical structure of the imperfect tense. Further, using cultural stories in a PACE lesson also provides a rich context for co-constructing in discussion with students the ways that grammar serves to make meaning in the story (see HLTP #4, Volume I).

One caveat is in order, however. Some textbooks today are designed to maintain the context throughout the chapter and relate all aspects of the chapter, such as vocabulary, cultural information, grammar, readings, and more to the overarching context. If this is the case, teachers need to be careful not to strip the grammar presentation of the context and default to teacher-fronted decontextualized explanations of grammar. As Cammarata (2010) noted in his well-documented study, many teachers believe in an idealized linear sequence of language instruction that maintains that competence is required before performance, so isolated language knowledge is frontloaded before language use and learning vocabulary and grammar takes priority with context relegated to a secondary instructional goal.

Donato (2016) has also discussed the challenge of integrating language and content and the problematic practice of pre-teaching grammar and vocabulary out of its context of use. As we will discuss in the next chapter, the grammar for a unit or series of lessons is selected only after the topic, inquiry question, and performance objectives have been identified, given that grammar is a tool that enables students to achieve the objectives. Teachers have agency, that is, decision-making power, to choose the grammatical structures that best serve the context of instruction; if some structures included in the textbook are not appropriate within a specific context, teachers can ignore or postpone them.

(5) *Should students be made aware of the context of a language lesson? Should the context be explicitly stated to students?* Yes, it is important to anchor a lesson in a context and to make this context explicit to students at the beginning of a unit and each lesson. Additionally, context should be unambiguous, developmentally appropriate, and easy for students to understand. When the context of the lesson is made clear to students, they will find it easier to grasp the information presented, will more easily map meanings onto forms, and will understand the purpose of the tasks that they are asked to perform. From the students' perspective, language lessons can be difficult to navigate. Students often find it difficult to understand why their teacher asks particular types of questions or assigns certain kinds of activities and tasks. Establishing contexts for

instruction cannot therefore be the unique purview of the teacher. Contexts must be shared with students and the reasons for working with each context made clear to them.

For example, after a class observation, a language program coordinator in a university second-semester class reported that the teacher designed a contextualized lesson based on changing roles of men and women over the years as part of a larger unit of study on gender equity. The teacher opened his class by asking the students who performed certain chores in their homes. Silence came over the class and no answer from students was forthcoming to this rather straightforward question. The problem was not that the students had nothing to say or were unmotivated, as some teachers might conclude. The problem was that the students were confused because the teacher did not make explicit that the context of the class for the next few days was to explore how gender roles have changed over the years. If he had done so, students would have more easily perceived the teacher's goal for beginning the lesson by asking them to state the roles that men and women have in their own families. If the context of the lesson had been clear to students, they most likely would have been able to offer their observations to the discussion rather than sit silently because the teacher's question appeared to come out of nowhere and be asked for no reason.

(6) *Context is complex and is shaped by many features. Do I need to ensure that all contextual elements are present in everything I teach or in every task or activity for the students?* Indeed, context is reflected in all aspects of each lesson and there should be some connection to a goal established by the inquiry question. However, not all aspects of the lesson need to specify every contextual element. One way to think of the amount of contextual information to provide is to think of a continuum from little contextual information to a detailed account of the context. The goal of instruction in a class guides decisions of what to provide in terms of contextual information. For example, if students are learning to perform a specific language function with the goal of developing their interactive competence (Hall, 1995), then as much information as possible about the features of the interaction should be provided.

Deconstructing the Practice

This high-leverage practice is deconstructed in terms of identifying the topic/theme, inquiry question, language functions, and grammar and vocabulary. At the conclusion of this section, Figure 7.1 depicts a tool designed to assist teachers in enacting this practice. As a reminder, the practices of carrying the context through instruction and assessment will be deconstructed in the following chapters.

Establishing a Meaningful and Purposeful Context (Stage 1 in Backward-Design Planning)

1. Identify the topic or theme of the lesson or unit. One way to begin to design supportive contexts for instruction is to identify a specific topic (e.g., nutrition, family, professions) or overarching theme (e.g., courage and heroism, prejudice, community) that will unite all aspects of the lesson or unit. Often curriculum materials and textbooks provide these kinds of topics or themes. Determine how the theme or topic is relevant to students and

will engage their interest at a level appropriate to their language abilities. Keep in mind that the topic or theme will become the framework for identifying a purposeful and meaningful goal for the inquiry question and for establishing all other aspects of the lesson, such as the presentation of new grammatical structures and vocabulary, interpersonal pair work tasks, oral or written presentational communication tasks, selection of print texts and media, and out-of-class projects. Although the topic or theme is insufficient for specifying the context in clear terms, it will nonetheless serve as the foundation and inspiration for establishing the question to explore, the purpose and goal for exploring the question, and the context for all other parts of the lesson.

2. Identify one inquiry question that drives the topic or theme. How will the general topic be used and serve as the focus for inquiry? What purposeful goal motivates the exploration of the topic or theme? In other words, what 'inquiry question' provides the rationale for exploring the topic or theme? An **inquiry question** could be an issue to investigate or a relevant and compelling problem to solve, not unlike the notion of the 'big idea' proposed by Wiggins and McTighe (2005). For example, this type of question can present an issue to investigate, as in "How have eating habits changed over the years?" or a problem to solve in which students express interest, as in "Should the school day start later?" Note that effective inquiry questions cannot be answered with one correct response, a "yes" or "no," or in a single sentence. Instead, appropriate inquiry questions are answered only by synthesizing information and the results of communicative exchanges (e.g., pair interviews, text-based discussions, interpretive reading, web searches) conducted over the course of the unit of instruction dealing with this particular context.

Additionally, the inquiry question needs to take into consideration what students can do with language at various levels of instruction and how their emerging language abilities can be used to investigate the question and to formulate responses. Asking an inquiry question that requires responses in language that students cannot possibly express at their level serves no purpose. Teachers are well aware of what their students can do with the target language and therefore should take this into consideration when posing inquiry questions.

An example of using an inquiry question to frame the topic/context is to begin with a common textbook or curriculum unit topic such as "nutrition." For reasons explored earlier, although this topic provides content, it does not provide much in terms of an actual context. However, we could approach this topic from the standpoint of the inquiry question, "How do cultural norms influence concepts of good nutrition?" This question could then become the framework for designing a series of connected lessons that allow students to explore texts and cross-cultural perspectives, engage in discussions, conduct research on the internet, compose opinions in writing, and focus on language that is relevant to the issue being explored. Planning for all parts of the unit or lesson around an inquiry question becomes clear and well defined in terms of who is speaking, the content of the talk-in-interaction, the roles of the speakers, the goals of the interaction, and the types of language functions to use for the speaking events. In sum, establishing a compelling question to explore may prevent the all too often asked student question, "Why are we learning this stuff, anyway?"

3. Identify the language functions of the lesson/unit and how they relate to the context. After having established the overarching topic of the lesson or unit (e.g., nutrition or transportation) as well as the inquiry question, identify the language functions that students will use and learn in this context. In some cases, textbook material or curriculum will specify these communicative functions. It is important to be clear on how the communication tasks that students will complete reflect the context in terms of the speakers, the setting or speech situation, the goals of the speaking event, and the type of language necessary for carrying out the function. For example, if the topic is transportation—and depending on the inquiry question—possible functions are asking a travel agent for the best option for traveling in the target language country, giving a friend advice on preferred modes of transportation in and around the city, discussing the best modes of transportation for different destinations, or sharing with classmates out-of-class research on the most energy efficient modes of transportation. Each of these functions implies several contextual factors about which students need to be aware—who is speaking, the nature of the communication (academic reporting vs. personal opinion), the goal of the communication (giving advice vs. asking for information), and the type of language students need to use to perform the functions in context (e.g., academic language, asking for information, stating a personal opinion, making an argument). To this end, the S-P-E-A-K-I-N-G Model presented earlier can be used to identify the language functions (or communicative acts) that are necessary for understanding and describing communicative situations in context.

Within the nutrition theme and the inquiry question "How do cultural norms influence concepts of good nutrition?" functions might include sharing opinions about popular diets, asking a friend about preferred nutritional habits, or comparing nutritional models across cultures (e.g., the U.S. Department of Agriculture food plate, Belgium or Italy's food triangle, Spain's food pyramid).

4. Identify the grammar and vocabulary relevant to the context. Grammar and vocabulary serve the context—i.e., they are selected as tools for making meaning and engaging in target-language interactions based on the context. In traditional approaches to language instruction, teachers begin planning with grammar and attempt to attach a context and speech events to it, which often results in artificially contrived situations in which grammatical structures are forced and not typically used in interactions beyond the classroom. What often happens, as Cammarata's (2010) and Donato's (2016) research has shown, is that teachers initially decontextualize the teaching of language elements, then expect students to integrate what was presented into later contextualized activities and tasks. By pre-teaching vocabulary or grammar out of context, sometimes called 'frontloading the lesson,' teachers make mapping meaning onto form more difficult and students are unable to see the relationship of what is presented to the larger goals and outcomes of the lesson, i.e., participation in various modes of communication. By way of analogy, pre-teaching language out of context is similar to making an actor rehearse discrete lines for a play without understanding how the lines connect to the character, story, or theme. The practice of decontextualized frontloading of new grammar or vocabulary information also destroys the lesson's coherence and results in a class that appears to be made up of random activities disconnected from each other with no apparent motivation for learning other than to demonstrate in-the-moment knowledge of language rules or vocabulary.

In the example of the unit on nutrition, grammatical structures in Spanish that might be useful would include present tense, noun/adjective agreement, expressions of comparisons (e.g., *más/menos* + adjective + que), and the subjunctive mood to express doubt or inquire about the existence of certain foods in a particular diet. Vocabulary would feature names of foods/ingredients/beverages, adjectives for describing how foods taste (e.g., salty, sweet, sour), names of diets and dietary restrictions, menu vocabulary, and words that denote measurements/quantities (e.g., kilo, cup, pound). It is important to realize that grammatical structures and vocabulary can be useful across multiple contexts and that selection of them depends on the nature of the speech situations and speech events (i.e., language functions) that are the focus, as well as new information to be acquired. For example, the present subjunctive mood in Spanish is used in a number of language functions such as expressing emotion or doubt, describing something that may not yet be found (such as a new house or job), making a statement about an event not within the speaker's control, or describing an event that might take place in the future. Consequently, this structure would be included in multiple contexts given that it serves multiple communicative purposes or functions. A similar case could be made for vocabulary, such as food vocabulary, which can be used for a variety of functions from naming foods needed for a party to debating which types of foods should be consumed to maintain a healthy diet. In sum, care needs to be taken to identify the *most useful* grammar and vocabulary necessary for exploring the inquiry question and performing communicative functions within the thematic focus.

Steps in Establishing a Context	Questions to Ask if Using a Textbook or Curriculum Guide
1. Identify the topic or theme of the lesson or unit.	Does the textbook or curriculum guide offer a context that is interesting, meaningful, unambiguous, and purposeful?
2. Identify one inquiry question that drives the topic or theme.	Does the context of the textbook or curriculum guide provide a real reason for learning the language beyond learning a grammar 'rule'? Is there a tangible outcome or goal relevant to the context that can move exploration of the content and context of instruction forward?
3. Identify the language functions of the lesson/unit and how they relate to the context.	Does the context of the textbook or curriculum guide allow for interactions in the target language that go beyond simple mechanical practice of language forms? Can students perceive that what will be learned is useful and reflects ways that language is used outside the classroom in everyday encounters?
4. Identify the grammar and vocabulary relevant to the context.	Are grammar and vocabulary presentations in the textbook or curriculum guide situated in the context? Do demonstrations and explanations illustrate how the grammar is used to make meaning in context?

Figure 7.1. **Tool for Establishing a Meaningful and Purposeful Context for Language Instruction**

Note: The questions in the second column are relevant for teachers who use a textbook or curriculum guide. A "yes" response should be accompanied by examples and a "no" response should indicate how the weakness will be addressed in creating the context.

Rehearsing the Practice

The following tasks provide ways to practice developing a meaningful context as the first stage of planning meaningful and communicative lessons and units.

1. Using the S-P-E-A-K-I-N-G model described in the Theory and Research section of this chapter, observe a two- to three- minute interaction from a film (e.g., a film trailer or talk show on YouTube) or in real life (e.g., a conversation at a meal, a conversation among friends, an exchange when purchasing an item), and describe the context of interaction by explaining as many of the components of the S-P-E-A-K-I-N-G model as you can based on your observational data. If parts of the context are unclear to you, explain why. Explain what you observed and share your observations with those in your pedagogy class or professional development session.

2. For each of the following speech situations, identify at least two communicative language functions expressed as a speaking event that could be observed. For example, if the speech situation is a party, one could observe a self-introduction to a person one does not know, individuals stating likes and dislikes about recent movies, or discussions about school, jobs, or leisure time activities. Share your language functions in context with others in your pedagogy class or professional development session.

- In a classroom
- At the mall
- At home watching TV with a friend
- At a job interview
- At the doctor's office

3. Using a language textbook, select and review an entire chapter/lesson in terms of Halliday's model. Describe the chapter's/lesson's field (what the chapter is about; what the content is); the tenor of interactions students will engage in based on activities provided (who is involved and what their roles are); and the mode or modes of communication that students will experience in the chapter (what language is used in these interactions and for what purpose—interpersonal, interpretive, or presentational communication). Be as comprehensive as possible in your analysis. Review introductory presentation of new vocabulary and grammar, readings, grammar explanations, whole class or pair work tasks, cultural contexts, and writing projects. Conclude with a personal evaluation of the chapter in terms of how a unified context was used (or not) as a framework for the chapter. If weaknesses are found, state how you might improve the chapter or what modifications you would make.

4. Select an exercise or activity from a textbook (preferably the one you use, if possible) that focuses on oral practice of a grammatical structure. Keeping in mind Walz's study on mechanical exercises that are framed in shallow and meaningless contexts, evaluate the exercise in terms of the information that is provided to the students on how language is used in the context of the exercise. Rate the exercise on a 3-point scale. A rating of 3 indicates that the exercise is highly contextualized, motivating, and clear on the nature of

the communication. A rating of 2 indicates that some context is provided but insufficient to clarify fully the use of language in context or to motivate students to complete the exercise. A rating of 1 indicates that no contextual information is provided to motivate the completion of the exercise or to identify how the forms used in the task are useful for meaning making beyond the immediate task. Explain the exercise you selected and your rating to those in your group.

5. Now develop your own context for a lesson or unit of instruction by identifying:

- The theme or topic
- The inquiry question
- Language functions related to the context (review the S-P-E-A-K-I-N-G Model presented earlier)
- Grammar and vocabulary relevant to the context
- Sample target-language interactions for students to complete in class
- One formative assessment task and one summative assessment task

To aid completion of this task, you may want to use External Mediational Tool #7 in Appendix 1-A.

6. Using the context you identified above, select five to seven thematically-related vocabulary words that reflect the context of instruction. Develop a presentation of these new vocabulary words in context and in extended discourse, that is, in a spoken text that is comprehensible and at an appropriate level for the class. The purpose of the lesson is to teach vocabulary in context and to support students' comprehension and production of the new lexical items. Simply asking for repetition of words after the teacher or presenting decontextualized single words is not allowed. Students' production of the new words must be achieved in context and must demonstrate their comprehension of each word's meaning. You may want to review ways to create comprehensible language in Chapter 1 of Volume I to prepare this vocabulary lesson for introducing the meaning and uses of the new words in a thematic or topical context.

7. Using the context you identified above, design a lesson focusing on grammatical form that will be a part of the unit or lesson; you may want to use the PACE Model presented in Volume I. Identify how the form is placed within the context and describe a speaking event that might require the grammatical form within this context. For example, the introduction of prepositions of location might be framed in the context of descriptions of the location of various places in your school or city to a newcomer; or learning about descriptive adjectives and agreement might be framed in the context of describing a famous painting from the target language culture and observing how attributes of individuals or objects reflect an artistic movement. Develop an interactive presentation of this new material in the context of the lesson. Explain the objective of your lesson followed by a demonstration of your lesson to your peers. Include any visuals you might need to support the introduction of the new material.

Assessing the Practice

Use Rubric #7 in Appendix 1-B to self-assess the context you developed in (5) above. As an alternative or in addition, you could ask a colleague to review a lesson that you have planned (and/or observe it) and provide feedback using the appropriate categories on the rubric.

Putting the Practice into a Larger Context: Instructional Goals and Challenges

Of all the concepts associated with the educational literature, teaching in context appears to be a high-leverage practice that is shared across all disciplines. The necessity of context is therefore incontestable in learning any new skill, information, or concept, and this would include learning a foreign language. By acknowledging the role of context in language instruction, foreign language education aligns with other academic areas and moves from a marginalized position in discussions of instructional practices. Although the discipline of language teaching has its own unique set of high-leverage practices, establishing meaningful and purposeful context for learning is one area in which colleagues can engage in mutually beneficial conversations across disciplines and learn from each other.

Why is context so important to the work of educators and why is the concept so pervasive in the educational literature? As discussed previously, context supports learning by making what is learned memorable, comprehensible, and transferable to the world outside the classroom. In this way, school-based learning is a special kind of learning that does not duplicate the world (as if the classroom ever could), but rather provides the necessary concepts and knowledge that allow students to deal with the world outside the classroom. Context is one way of ensuring that what students learn and do in classrooms is relevant, useful, and transferable to their lives.

Colleagues in other subject areas also perceive the need for highly contextualized lessons in academic settings to support student learning and to show the relevance of what is learned to real world problems and issues. For example, in reading and language arts education, Beck, McKeown, and Kucan (2002) present several contextualized strategies for developing robust vocabulary knowledge and for assisting students in making use of context cues to derive meaning when reading. Based on the research, they argue that using context to derive meaning needs to be taught and cannot be assumed to emerge naturally. Based on research on the reasoning processes of students as they worked with context to derive meaning (see, for example, McKeown, 1985), they argue that, left to their own devices, some learners make limited use of context or, conversely, go beyond the context and invent scenarios to justify how meaning might fit the context of a text. McKeown (1985) concludes that vocabulary instruction needs to focus on the *process* of deriving meaning directly from context rather than on the *product* of arriving at an accurate meaning of an unknown word.

Mathematics education has embraced contextualized instruction for grounding the teaching of mathematics in relevant issues that are part of students' lives (National Council of Teachers of Mathematics [NCTM], 2014). The Australian Mathematics Society Institute (AMSI) maintains that mathematics instruction must make use of real-world contexts. Contextualized mathematics instruction is critical to engaging students in mathematical thinking and serves as a key catalyst for developing mathematical understandings. It may surprise language teachers to learn that AMSI also proposes the use of stories (personal experiences, anecdotes, videos, and stories that involve the use of numbers) to introduce new topics and areas of study. Smith and Stein (2011), in their book *5 Practices for Orchestrating Productive Mathematics Discussions*, offer a detailed guide for connecting mathematical problem solving to rich tasks that are meaningful and purposeful to students and that lead to discussions that make student thinking and reasoning visible to the class. The authors also argue for the need to offer students compelling and interesting questions, much like the inquiry questions presented in this chapter, which can be answered in a multitude of ways, rather than straightforward, one-right-answer questions that are unlikely to lead to engagement with tasks and group discussion.

Finally, curriculum innovation in science education has proposed connecting the learning of science concepts to solving local problems in the students' communities that are connected to their experiences and reality (Cook & Quigley, 2013). Cook and Quigley found in their study of university students' use of the method Photovoice that students appreciated connecting scientific concepts to the context of environmental issues of interest to them on campus. As they had hypothesized, when scientific inquiry was contextualized in environmental problems and potential solutions facing the local campus community, students quickly became engaged with caring about the issues, deepened their understanding of underlying scientific principles, and showed enthusiasm in carrying out their semester projects. Additionally, the use of Photovoice allowed students to present the issue visually as it related to their lives and in the context of relevant and understandable problems of the campus community.

In summary, the concept of context and contextualizing instruction is an area that reveals common ground that foreign language education shares with several other academic disciplines and instructional approaches. Research in other subject areas has revealed that teaching content in context matters and results in robust instruction for reading and interpreting texts, engaging in meaningful classroom discussions, and solving problems dealing with the world outside the classroom, among other advantages. Foreign language learning is no exception. But to enact this high-leverage practice requires understanding deeply the meaning of context and how it serves as the overarching framework of lessons and units of study. Further, it requires moving beyond understanding context as shallow settings and generic statements about language to fully articulating goals for what and how teachers will teach and what students will learn to do in their new language.

References

Beck, I. L., McKeown, M. G., & Kucan, L. (2002). *Bringing words to life: Robust vocabulary instruction.* New York: Guilford.

Byrnes, H. (2009). Systemic-functional reflections on instructed foreign language acquisition as meaning-making: An introduction. *Linguistics and Education, 20*(1), 1-9.

Cammarata, L. (2010). Foreign language teachers' struggles to learn content-based instruction. *L2 Journal, 2*(1), 89-118.

Clementi, D., & Terrill, L. (2013). *The keys to planning for learning.* Alexandria, VA: ACTFL.

Cook, K., & Quigley, C. (2013). Connecting to our community: Using Photovoice as a pedagogical tool to connect students to science. *International Journal of Environmental and Science Education, 8*(2), 339-357.

Donato, R. (2016). Sociocultural theory and content-based foreign language instruction: Theoretical insights on the challenge of integration. In L. Cammarata (Ed.), *Content-based foreign language teaching: Curriculum and pedagogy for developing advanced thinking and literacy skills* (pp. 25-50). New York: Routledge.

Glisan, E. W., & Donato, R. (2017). *Enacting the work of language instruction: High-leverage teaching practices.* Alexandria, VA: ACTFL.

Hall, J. K. (1995) 'Aw, man, where we goin?': Classroom interaction and the development of L2 interactional competence. *Issues in Applied Linguistics, 6,* 37-62.

Halliday, M. A. K. (2014). *Halliday's introduction to functional grammar* (4th ed.). New York: Routledge.

Hymes, D. (1972). Models of the interaction of language and social life. In J. Gumperz & D. Hymes (Eds.), *Directions in sociolinguistics: The ethnography of communication* (pp. 35-71). New York: Holt, Rhinehart & Winston.

Hymes, D. (1974). *Foundations in sociolinguistics: An ethnographic approach.* Philadelphia: University of Pennsylvania Press.

Larsen-Freeman, D. (2003). *Teaching language: From grammar to grammaring.* Boston: Heinle.

McKeown, M. G. (1985). The acquisition of word meaning from context by children of high and low ability. *Reading Research Quarterly, 20*(4), 482-496.

National Council of Teachers of Mathematics (NCTM). (2014). *Principles to actions: Ensuring mathematical success for all.* Reston, VA: Author.

National Standards Collaborative Board. (2015). *World-readiness standards for learning languages* (4th ed.). Alexandria, VA: Author.

Shrum, J. L., & Glisan, E. W. (2016). *Teacher's handbook: Contextualized language instruction.* Boston: Cengage.

Smith, M. S., & Stein, M. K. (2011). *5 practices for orchestrating productive mathematics discussions.* Reston, VA: NCTM.

Sousa, D. A. (2011). *How the brain learns* (4th ed.). Thousand Oaks, CA: Corwin.

van Compernolle, R. A. (2015). *Interaction and second language development: A Vygotskian perspective.* Amsterdam: John Benjamins. https://doi.org/10.1075/lllt.44

Van Lier, L. (1996). *Interaction in the language curriculum: Awareness, autonomy, and authenticity.* New York: Longman.

Walz, J. (1989). Context and contextualized language practice in foreign language teaching. *Modern Language Journal, 73,* 161-168.

Wiggins, G., & McTighe, J. (2005). *Understanding by design.* Alexandria, VA: ASCD.

Young, R. F. (2008). *Language and interaction: An advanced resource book.* New York: Routledge.

Appendix 1-A

External Mediational Tool #7: Establishing a Meaningful and Purposeful Context for Language Instruction

Note: The questions in the second column are relevant for teachers who use a textbook or curriculum guide. A "yes" response should be accompanied by examples and a "no" response should indicate how the weakness will be addressed in creating the context.

Steps in Establishing a Context	Questions to Ask if Using a Textbook or Curriculum Guide
1. Identify the topic or theme of the lesson or unit.	Does the textbook or curriculum guide offer a context that is interesting, meaningful, unambiguous, and purposeful?
2. Identify one inquiry question that drives the topic or theme.	Does the context of the textbook or curriculum guide provide a real reason for learning the language beyond learning a grammar 'rule'? Is there a tangible outcome or goal relevant to the context that can move exploration of the content and context of instruction forward?
3. Identify the language functions of the lesson/unit and how they relate to the context.	Does the context of the textbook or curriculum guide allow for interactions in the target language that go beyond simple mechanical practice of language forms? Can students perceive that what will be learned is useful and reflects ways that language is used outside the classroom in everyday encounters?
4. Identify the grammar and vocabulary relevant to the context.	Are grammar and vocabulary presentations in the textbook or curriculum guide situated in the context? Do demonstrations and explanations illustrate how the grammar is used to make meaning in context?

Appendix 1-B

Rubric for HLTP #7: Establishing a Meaningful and Purposeful Context for Language Instruction

	Exceeds Expectations	**Meets Expectations**	**Developing**	**Unacceptable**
Nature of Context: Meaningful, Purposeful in Learning Goals and Objectives	Context is meaningful and has a clear purpose in learning goals and objectives. Context motivates learners to want to learn and interact in the target language.	Context is meaningful and has a clear purpose in learning goals and objectives.	Context is meaningful but lacks purpose in learning goals and objectives.	Context is superficial and lacks meaning and/or purpose in learning goals and objectives. Context may be from a textbook or curriculum guide with no adaptations to make it meaningful/ purposeful.
Scope of Context	Context is driven by a larger goal or inquiry question that presents an issue to investigate or a problem to solve.	Context makes connections to a larger goal or inquiry question that presents an issue to investigate or a problem to solve.	Context makes connections to a larger goal but lacks an inquiry question that presents an issue to investigate or a problem to solve.	Context provides a topic or theme but is not related to a larger goal or inquiry question.
Connection of Context to Language Functions	Context is anchored to specific language functions that include speech events, speakers, goals, language necessary to carry out speech events.	Context identifies specific language functions that include speech events, speakers, goals, language necessary to carry out speech events.	Context identifies specific language functions that include several but not all of the following aspects: speech events, speakers, goals, language necessary to carry out speech events.	Context lacks a connection to specific language functions.
Relevance of Grammar and Vocabulary to Context	Selected grammar and vocabulary are essential tools for the context, including the inquiry question and language functions, and are taught within the context.	Selected grammar and vocabulary are taught within the context.	Most of the grammar and vocabulary are taught within the context. Or either the grammar or vocabulary is taught within the context, but not both.	Grammar and vocabulary tend to be taught (or 'pre-taught') out of context, and/ or grammar and vocabulary are from a textbook and lack a connection to the context.

CHAPTER 2

HLTP #8: Planning for Instruction Using an Iterative Process for Backward Design

By beginning the planning process with clearly specified outcomes, planning aligns itself with current foreign language professional initiatives that emphasize actual language performances that are transferable beyond immediate classroom instruction.

Few would dispute the claim that knowledge of how to plan for instruction is a requisite skill that all teachers should possess in order to effect student learning. In fact, research has documented the unfortunate state in which many novice teachers find themselves as a result of not knowing what to teach or how to teach it, particularly in the absence of clearly defined goals and desired results (see, for example, Jones, Jones, & Vermette, 2011; Kauffman, Johnson, Kardos, Liu, & Peske, 2002). One study labeled new teachers as being 'lost at sea' where lesson planning is concerned (Kauffman, Johnson, Kardos, Liu, & Peske, 2002). Other studies "show many new teachers struggling with curriculum either on a basic level—figuring out what and how to teach—or on a more conceptual level—negotiating the curriculum frameworks, pre-packaged programs, and district guidelines that they find in their new positions" (Graff, 2011, p. 152).

The HLTP explored in this chapter seeks to deconstruct and detail the complex practice of planning for instruction. To this end, the discussion in Chapter 1 explored the pivotal role of context in designing lessons and units of instruction. Using context as the overarching concept, teachers must make decisions about how to organize and plan contextualized learning experiences that enable students to achieve desired outcomes. Planning is a complex teaching practice that includes knowledge of subject matter and professional standards, an understanding of students and how they learn (e.g., their backgrounds, previous learning experiences, levels of proficiency in the target language, specific learning needs), course and curricular goals, research-based pedagogical practices, and ways in which students will be assessed to provide evidence of learning (Graff, 2011; Shulman, 1986). For this reason, if teachers are to gain control of planning, its complexity needs to be made visible and not reduced to jargon or generalities about the process.

For well over a decade, the field of education has embraced an approach to planning that begins with the identification of the desired outcomes of instruction, which are subsequently used to drive assessment design and then instructional experiences, in what is referred to as a 'backward design' (Wiggins & McTighe, 2005). As will be discussed in further detail later, this type of approach contrasts with an approach to planning in which learning experiences (e.g., activities, tasks, presentations) are planned first based on loosely specified linguistic objectives and in which decisions regarding assessment occur at the end of instruction.

This chapter features planning within a backward-design approach as a high-leverage practice given its critical role in the current state of the profession, which values and places an emphasis on outcomes (e.g., proficiency) and the types of evidence that confirm what learners are able to do with the target language. The model of planning proposed here as an HLTP begins and ends with the inquiry question in context, initially by posing a relevant and interesting question that launches and frames instruction, and finally, by assessing the degree to which learners have been able to provide thoughtful responses in the target language that adequately address the scope of the question. However, this HLTP goes beyond the backward-design framework of Wiggins and McTighe (2005) by featuring planning as an iterative process in which work on one stage of the backward planning may necessitate a return to a previous stage to make changes in the plan. This iterative process for a backward design approach to planning recognizes and respects the way that students learn languages in classroom settings, the mediated nature of language learning and development, and an approach to instruction that supports student success in classrooms.

ACTFL/CAEP Standards addressed: #3a, #3b, #4a, #4b, #5a

Research and Theory Supporting the Practice

Approaches to Planning in Language Teaching

In the literature on curriculum development, syllabus design, and lesson planning, the approach most often described, be it in foreign language or in other academic disciplines such as math, science, social studies, and English language arts, is labeled 'backward design.' However, Richards (2013) describes three different approaches to planning in language education, each of which has enjoyed a certain degree of popularity based on evolving understandings of language instruction: 'forward design,' 'central design,' and 'backward design.' Each of these entails a different understanding of the relationships among elements that Richards refers to as input, process, and output. These terms should not be confused with those used in second language acquisition, as Richards uses them in a different manner within the context of language instruction. According to Richards, **input** refers to the linguistic content of a course; **process** is the methodology used to carry out teaching and includes the types of learning activities and strategies employed by teachers; and **output** relates to learning outcomes, or what learners can do with the language as a result of instruction (Richards, 2013, pp. 6-7). In this regard, the three different approaches to planning reflect different understandings of the nature of language and language learning; the roles of teachers, learners, and instructional materials; and the intended outcomes of learning—i.e., knowledge and performance. In what follows, these three approaches to planning will be discussed as background and as a way to contrast backward design with other approaches. The HLTP in this chapter will focus, however, on a backward-planning design and the reasons why backward planning is consistent with today's goals for language instruction.

Forward design assumes that input, process, and output have a linear relationship; that is, when planning units of instruction and component lessons, the contents of instruction are identified before decisions are made about methodology and output. In typical forward-design unit and lesson planning, for example, the teacher chooses a topic, selects instructional methods and resources, and then creates an assessment to check understanding and/or evaluate performance. According to Richards, forward planning may be an option when "the aims of learning are understood in very general terms" such as in language courses where goals are described in terms of "proficiency in language use across a wide range of daily situations" or "communicative ability in the four language skills" (2013, p. 9). Two examples of specific approaches in language teaching that supported a forward design in planning include the Audiolingual Method (ALM), popular in the 1960s and based on behaviorism and stimulus-response learning (Lado, 1964); and Communicative Language Teaching (CLT), which appeared in the late 1970s and proposed the communicative syllabus focused on language as social actions as a replacement for the traditional grammatical syllabus model (Littlewood, 1981; Munby, 1978; Nunan, 1991; Richards 2006; Savignon, 1987).

Richards uses the label **central design** to describe planning that begins with teaching activities, techniques, and methods instead of a detailed description of content or learning outcomes. According to research on teaching practices, teachers who initiate their planning by contemplating the types of activities and exercises they will use in the classroom (that is, the process rather than the input or the output) follow a central design approach. The central design approach leaves open the possibility that students, as shapers of their learning, may take instruction in unanticipated directions based on their own self-selected learning goals. This approach also gives teachers greater responsibility for creating their own curriculum and lessons in the classroom. Examples of language teaching methods initiated in the late 1970s and 1980s that prompted a central design to planning are the Natural Approach (Terrell, 1982), the Silent Way (Gattegno, 1976), and Community Language Learning (Curran, 1976). In a central design approach to planning, "learning is not viewed as the mastery of pre-determined content but as constructing new knowledge through participating in specific learning and social contexts and through engaging in particular types of activities and processes" (Richards, 2013, p. 19).

In contrast to forward and central design, **backward design** begins with a detailed description of the desired outcomes of instruction, with assessments and teaching experiences planned after intended instructional outcomes have been articulated. Many language educators are familiar with the application of backward design popularized by Wiggins and McTighe's (2005) work on this approach in language arts, math, science, and social studies. The approach to backward design presented in this chapter is based in part on the work of Wiggins and McTighe, research that has been conducted on this model of planning, and experiences with novice teachers learning the approach and applying it. As will be discussed later in the chapter, the Wiggins and McTighe model has been modified in this HLTP given that it is not entirely transferable to the foreign language context.

The change from traditional teacher-centered classrooms where the teacher is only the dispenser and assessor of knowledge to classrooms in which teachers assist students toward the accomplishment of clearly defined learning targets at various levels of instruction is supported by backward design. In this regard, when engaging in a backward-design approach to planning, several important factors affecting language learning need to be kept in mind: the specification of level-appropriate learner performances in the three modes of communication, assessments on real world tasks, interdisciplinary content, the interconnectedness of language and culture, language use in context, and learners as active meaning makers assisted by teachers who guide, motivate, and assist them through interactions and instructional conversations, to name a few (see Shrum & Glisan, 2015, Chapter 3).

Across all academic areas and levels of instruction, backward design specifies and requires the following three steps to planning:

1. Identify desired learning outcomes.
2. Determine acceptable evidence of learning.
3. Plan learning experiences and instruction (Richards, 2013, p. 18).

Backward planning is not new, despite its rise in popularity in an era of instructional accountability. Richards notes that "backward design was a well-established tradition in curriculum design in general education" (2013, p. 20) dating back to Tyler, who proposed the use of objectives in instructional planning in 1949, and explained:

> Educational objectives become the criteria by which materials are selected, content is outlined, instructional procedures are developed, and tests and examinations are prepared. . . . The purpose of a statement of objectives is to indicate the kinds of changes in the student to be brought about so that instructional activities can be planned and developed in a way likely to attain these objectives. (Tyler, 1949, quoted in Richards, 2013, p. 21)

Even earlier than the work of Tyler, Polya (1945) discussed the benefits of "thinking backward" as a problem-solving strategy that dated back to the Greeks: "...it does not take a genius to solve a concrete problem working backwards; anyone can do it with a little common sense. We concentrate on the desired end, we visualize the final position in which we would like to be. From what foregoing position could we get there?" (p. 230)

Richards notes that the backward-design planning option may be particularly useful in situations that require a high degree of accountability, that is, those in which learners must meet stated outcomes as a prerequisite for further study, to attain a credential, or to advocate for and provide evidence to stakeholders in support of a language program.

One of the early disciplines to adopt a backward-design approach was STEM (science, technology, engineering, mathematics), inasmuch as the desired outcomes became the launching point for course design (Davidovitch, 2013; Streveler, Smith, & Pilotte, 2012). Other disciplines at PK-16 levels soon embraced this framework as well, including academic writing (Deane & O'Neill, 2011), information literacy instruction (Talley, 2014), pharmacy education (Daugherty, 2006), and foreign language education (Shrum & Glisan, 2016). Additionally, backward design has been proposed as the basis for developing "course-based undergraduate research experiences" (CUREs) (Cooper, Soneral, & Brownell, 2017, p.1) and for educational research design through a framework labeled 'Backward Design in Education Research' (BDER) (Jensen, Bailey, Kummer, & Weber, 2017). Beyond the field of education, this approach is used in professions such as engineering (Sheu & Chen, 2007), and business (Andreasen, 1985), in which designs for organizing and conducting work are based on desired end products.

Research on Backward Design

Research in education has pointed to the benefits of establishing desired outcomes before instruction begins (Davidovitch, 2013; Jones, Vermette, & Jones, 2009; Wiggins & McTighe, 2005). First, this enables both teachers and students to focus their efforts more effectively on the content and context that address the learning outcomes. Second, students become more active participants in the learning process by being able to assess their own knowledge and performance outcomes and can seek assistance to reach their goals. Third, backward design promotes an analysis of learners' prior knowledge, interests, and goals so that teachers can differentiate instruction for all learners, a critical element in effective planning. Fourth, beginning with clearly defined outcomes can ensure that the assessment matches the intended learning outcomes. Finally, with the desired outcomes in mind, teachers can analyze and evaluate their own teaching, identify areas that need improvement, and make necessary changes to their practice to bring about effective student learning (Stiggins, 2008).

Backward design-based planning stands in contrast to a teacher-centered approach to instruction, in which the teacher imparts information, then assesses only students' ability to remember and reproduce the content of the lesson. Backward design promotes the active involvement of learners and hence the development of metacognitive abilities so that learning becomes more than recall (Davidovitch, 2013). In this regard, according to research studies, students who experience learner-centered instruction through the teacher's use of a backward-design approach that keeps the students at the center of the plan have been found to be more knowledgeable about the topic explored, have more positive attitudes about learning, and feel in greater control of their grades (Harpe, Phipps, & Alowayesh, 2012). Additionally, there is some evidence to suggest that backward planning and making outcomes visible to students during instruction enable students to establish and satisfy their own personal achievement goals, which in turn motivates them in their study of languages (Korotchenko, Matveenko, Strelnikova, & Phillips, 2015).

Over the past decade, a body of research has confirmed that backward design is regarded by teachers as a valuable tool that enables them to plan with confidence. Graff (2011) conducted a qualitative study with new teachers to determine the extent to which the backward-design framework had been useful to them in teaching and to discover which aspects of the framework were particularly helpful. Out of 26 total respondents, 69% (18 teachers) indicated that they felt prepared to engage in planning after completion of a teacher preparation program and 65% referred specifically to the principles of backward design in justifying their degree of preparation to plan. Teachers attributed the ability to support students' success to their implementation of the backward-design framework, with one teacher commenting, "I need to know what I want my students to know and why I want them to know it before I teach it to them" (Graff, 2011, p. 162). Another interesting reflection in survey comments was the notion that students often commented on how organized their teachers appeared: "I got positive feedback from the kids about how organized I seemed and I always seemed to think I knew where I was going, so they thought that they knew where they were going" (p. 163). This reaction underscores how backward planning is not isolated to teacher actions but has a consequence in how students perceive the teacher and the teacher's commitment to their learning. One of the respondents expressed the opinion that she felt more confident in planning than did other new teachers at her school, "...who are just treading water every day and trying not to drown and don't really know what to do tomorrow" (p. 163). Beyond issues of planning, the Graff study revealed that teachers considered backward design as a tool for assessing and improving their teaching as well as for evaluating the quality of instructional materials.

In a self-reflective piece on how backward design changed her instruction, Fuglei (2015) noted that, prior to implementing this approach, she placed too much emphasis on content and too little focus on student understanding. Analysis of student work samples revealed that students exhibited only a superficial control of skills and an inability to demonstrate skills over the long term. In her view, backward design enabled her to focus on specific learning outcomes and adjust her teaching during the course of instruction to keep it aligned with these outcomes. Similarly, Herro (2018) recently examined the perceptions of teachers concerning the influence of professional development dealing with backward design on the effectiveness of curriculum development and implementation of planning instructional outcomes, assessments, and learning activities. Teachers reported that the backward design of plans based on learning objectives enabled them to maximize coverage of content, and further, that student understanding of learning goals was enhanced through formative feedback (including assessment rubrics) and classroom activities aligned with the goals.

Several studies revealed the positive impact of backward design as a framework for planning foreign language courses, curriculum, and programs. A recent study examined the use of the backward-design approach in re-conceptualizing an introductory undergraduate French curriculum to overcome the challenges of what has long been referred to as the 'language-literature divide' in post-secondary language programs (Byrnes, Maxim, & Norris, 2010; Modern Language Association Ad Hoc Committee on Foreign Languages, 2007). In this project, described by Paesani, the backward-design model was used "to build the program from the bottom up, determine programmatical objectives at the outset of the [curriculum] revision project and the tools used to measure them, and plan appropriate learning experiences consistent with our literacy-based approach" (2017, p. 9). Among the results of this study, students reported recognizing the connection between their classroom experiences in the introductory French course sequence and their attainment of stated learning objectives. Paesani's experience in this program revision led her to conclude that backward design serves as an effective tool to instructors for designing courses and curricula, provides stakeholders (e.g., instructors, students, administrators) with a roadmap that charts where the curriculum is leading, contributes to buy-in of faculty to course and program revision, and helps to avert the problem of regarding the textbook as the curriculum instead of as one resource (2007, p. 10). Finally, as a result of the backward approach to the redesign of this curriculum, assessment results and student feedback were used by instructors to make changes to the courses in the undergraduate French program and assessments as courses were being taught—that is, assessment results informed and improved teaching in a cyclical and dynamic manner. This finding will be taken up later in the chapter when explaining in more detail and deconstructing HLTP #8.

Two research studies relate to backward design and its impact on student learning in foreign language classes. Hodaeian and Biria (2015) examined the effectiveness of the backward-design model on the L2 reading comprehension of intermediate learners of English as a foreign language (EFL). Their study revealed that this model significantly impacted learners' reading comprehension skill and was also found to be a more effective planning option than the traditional forward design used for teaching reading comprehension. In another study, Korotchenko, Matveenko, Strelnikova, and Phillips (2015) reported on the successful implementation of backward design in the foreign language curriculum in the

Russian system of higher education. They found that students were more motivated to learn foreign languages because they felt that their own learning needs and goals had been met in a curriculum that focused on learning outcomes.

The Role of Backward Design in Foreign Language Education and Current Language Initiatives

In recent years, foreign language education, not unlike other subject areas, has paid increasing attention to accountability. As a result, virtually all pedagogical materials and professional guidelines for foreign language learning are written based on instructional goals and desired student outcomes of lessons, units, curriculum, programs of study, and even assessments. That is, authors of these documents have followed the principles of backward design by keeping desired outcomes in focus. For example, backward design has been suggested as the framework for instruction linked to the authentic performance tasks of the Integrated Performance Assessment (IPA) (Adair-Hauck, Glisan, & Troyan, 2013; Sandrock, 2010).

Because of the professional support that backward planning has received, instructors now have at their disposal a variety of detailed tools that can assist in implementing it, including the tool presented in the Deconstruction section of this chapter (Clementi & Terrill, 2013; Shrum & Glisan, 2016). The tools described below pertain both to language proficiency expectations and standards for language learning and can serve as the impetus for backward design in the contemporary foreign language classroom. To this end, they have established the desired instructional outcomes in terms of student performance, which language educators then use as the basis for creating assessments and engaging in planning at both the macro level (e.g., curricula, course syllabi) and micro level (e.g., unit and lesson plans).

First, the *ACTFL Proficiency Guidelines* (American Council on the Teaching of Foreign Languages [ACTFL], 2012b), which have a 40-year history in the United States and are well known by language professionals, delineate performance outcomes, whether attained in the classroom or in the world beyond the classroom. For example, speakers at the Intermediate-Mid level are able to participate in "...predictable and concrete exchanges necessary for survival in the target culture. These include personal information related to self, family, home, daily activities, interests and personal preferences, as well as physical and social needs, such as food, shopping, travel, and lodging" (ACTFL, 2012b, p. 7). Similarly, proficiency expectations are used beyond the United States in the Common European Framework of Reference for Languages (CEFR) (Council of Europe, 2001), which describes three levels of achievement (Basic User, Independent User, Proficient User) in terms of what learners should be able to do in reading, listening, speaking, and writing at each level. In this framework, one characteristic of an Independent User in terms of conversation as stated in the CEFR is "Can express and respond to feelings such as surprise, happiness, sadness, interest, and indifference" (quoted in Richards, 2013, p. 27). These expectations are then used as the basis for designing course syllabi, curriculum guidelines, assessments, and textbooks across Europe.

Second, backward design is also at the center of the *World-Readiness Standards for Learning Languages* (National Standards Collaborative Board, 2015). These standards describe what learners should know and be able to do as a result of language study across five broader goal areas: Communication, Cultures, Connections, Comparisons, and Communities. An example of an outcome for the Cultures goal area, for instance, is that "Learners use the language to investigate, explain, and reflect on the relationship between the practices and perspectives of the cultures studied" (National Standards Collaborative Board, 2015, p. 72). Although this is a broad statement of the goal of language instruction, it can serve as a guide in formulating outcomes in the initial stages of backward planning (see HLTP #5, Volume I).

Third, several documents derived from the standards can also inform a backward design to planning learning outcomes of instruction:

- The *21st Century Skills Map for World Languages* (Partnership for 21st Century Skills, 2011) illustrates how 21st century skills involving information, media, and technology intersect with world language standards and language proficiency.
- The *ACTFL Performance Descriptors for Language Learners* (ACTFL, 2012a) delineate three ranges of performance—Novice, Intermediate, Advanced—as benchmarks for learners who begin language learning at various ages/grade levels and who experience language study sequences of various lengths of time.
- The *NCSSFL-ACTFL Can-Do Statements* (ACTFL, 2013) represent checklists that language learners can use to assess what they 'can do' with the language in the three modes of communication and at various levels of proficiency.

In sum, given the outcome-driven perspective that permeates recent materials and professional publications, a backward-design approach to planning makes good sense as a way to realize what the profession supports as worthwhile and effective language instruction. Moreover, by beginning the planning process with clearly specified outcomes, planning aligns itself with current foreign language professional initiatives that emphasize actual language performances that are transferable beyond immediate classroom instruction.

Considerations about Engaging in Backward-Design Planning

(1) *Is backward design only applicable to PK-12 levels of instruction?* Backward-design planning is appropriate for *all* levels of instruction. Evidence to support its implementation at various levels of instruction was presented earlier and included its application in several academic areas and fields from elementary school to graduate programs in universities and colleges. As many teachers know, a backward-design approach to planning has enjoyed popularity in some pre-college settings. Applying backward design to university and college foreign language programs has also been undertaken partly in response to the report issued by the MLA Ad Hoc Committee on Foreign Languages. This report recommended that "graduate studies [in foreign language departments] should provide substantive training in language teaching" in response to the need for college faculty to develop expertise in language instruction (2007, p. 7). The research study reported on above that re-conceptualized the undergraduate French program provides evidence of the use of backward planning in post-secondary settings (Paesani, 2017). Similarly, Michael and Libarkin (2016) document a faculty member's pedagogical training in backward design to design and implement a college biology course.

They conclude that the training in backward design enabled the instructor to create a student-centered course and, further, that the close mentoring that the instructor received during training resulted in greater confidence in the ability to plan with this type of approach.

In another study, Davidovitch (2013) conducted a case study on backward design in STEM courses. Her findings led her to recommended that this approach be used in other subject areas as well. Davidovitch argued that when courses remain only content-focused, they result in disciplinary knowledge becoming irrelevant to students. She found that backward planning in STEM courses established learning outcomes and performances that required students to apply STEM course content to real world problems that were not considered when planning using the programs' routine planning model. She concluded that educators must strive for learning outcomes to drive instructional planning not only in STEM disciplines, but also in all other academic disciplines, including the humanities (Davidovitch, 2013, p. 334). The other studies reported on above documented successful results in implementing backward-design planning at post-secondary levels (Hodaeian & Biria, 2015; Korotchenko, Matveenko, Strelnikova, & Phillips, 2015; Paesani, 2017).

(2) *How is backward design realized in a daily lesson plan that is part of a larger thematic unit of study?* As is the case with larger thematic units, daily lesson plans reflect backward design inasmuch as the desired outcomes are identified first, followed by a determination of acceptable evidence that outcomes were attained, and then finally the planning of the learning experience. When creating daily lesson plans, consideration needs to be given to how the daily lesson fits into the larger unit of study that extends across days and perhaps weeks, and further, how each plan reflects the context of the unit and leads learners to answer the inquiry question by the end of the unit. Daily lesson plans are a component of the ultimate learning outcomes of a unit of study as specified in the first stage of backward design and play an important role in scaffolding students toward success. As such, daily lesson plans link to lessons that have come before and anticipate instruction in the future. In this way, teachers create a **zone of proximal development** (ZPD) by planning daily instruction based on what students know (students' actual level of development) with a view to where they are headed in their language development (potential level of development) through teacher assistance and mediation.

In backward design of daily lessons, learning experiences are sequenced so that one task or activity builds on the previous one and leads to the next within the context established in the first stage of planning. Regardless of the language level of learners, this sequencing does not mean that students first repeat memorized language void of context and then later proceed to more meaningful language use. Instead, all learning experiences should reflect meaning and relevancy within the context of the unit. Even novice learners can use the language they are learning to engage in meaningful and communicative tasks such as summarizing an authentic text or story, comparing cultural practices, conducting interviews of peers, or sharing opinions about a topic.

(3) *Are there research findings that inform the planning of daily lessons?* Neuroscience research provides a few guiding principles for teachers engaging in backward planning for the daily lesson plan. One example is the **primacy-recency effect**. The primacy-re-

cency effect means that, during a single lesson, learners remember best what comes first, they remember second best what comes last, and they remember least well what occurs just past the middle or during down-time (Gazzaniga, Ivry, & Mangun, 2002; Stephane et al., 2010). Hence, what is most important should be presented first in the lesson (e.g., new material) (Sousa, 2011). This approach to planning daily instruction therefore avoids using the first part of the lesson for typical classroom management tasks such as taking roll and making announcements. Correcting and collecting homework assignments is another activity that commonly occurs early in daily lessons. The primacy-recency effect suggests that the plan for the daily lesson should consider whether the homework assignment relates directly to the most important part of the daily lesson, such as the learning of new material or a new skill. If homework cannot be used at the start of the lesson to launch new material and motivate learners about the topic of the lesson, other ways of holding students accountable for completing homework assignments should be designed. In a similar vein, a productive use of the last part of the lesson—which learners remember second best—would be to conduct a lesson closure in which learners use the new information/skills or summarize what they have learned.

The findings of research in neuroscience have shown that **meaning** and **relevancy** are the features that have the most impact on understanding and retention of the material to be learned, be it grammar, vocabulary, cultural information, or functional uses of the language (Ausubel, 2012; Maquire, Frith, & Morris, 1999). This finding underscores the importance of planning for daily learning experiences that have a meaningful context and a purpose that students perceive as relevant and related to their lives (see HLTPs in Volume I and HLTP #7 in this volume). Further, these studies have found that the brain is activated when encountering **novel situations**, i.e., unpredictable events and circumstances that capture learners' attention (Weierich, Wright, Negreira, Dickerson, & Barrett, 2010). Integrating a degree of novelty into the daily lesson (e.g. humor, music, physical movement by students, a variety of pair work and collaborative tasks, and multisensory instruction using technology, visuals, manipulatives) is an effective way to focus student attention on the lesson content and the new language elements that constitute this content (Kennedy, 2006; Shrum & Glisan, 2016; Sousa, 2011).

(4) *How can I plan for target language use and classroom discourse during instruction as part of the backward-planning process?* In addition to the factors described above that shape and affect the planning process, planning for target language (TL) use and classroom discourse is also pivotal. Use of the TL during instruction can be planned and anticipated and, as suggested in the well-known position statement published by ACTFL in 2010, should be present for at least 90% of instructional time (see HLTP #1 in Volume I). Accordingly, teachers can plan in advance for the specific ways to make their TL comprehensible to learners during various learning experiences. Planning for comprehension-building strategies (see HLTP #1 and tool) is essential given the challenges that students may experience during lessons taught for the majority of the time in the TL. Additionally, planning and anticipating parts of the lesson that students may find difficult to comprehend avoids needing to decide 'in the moment' how to address students' comprehension difficulties. Similarly, planning ways to promote

talk-in-interaction through the use of IRF (see HLTP #2 in Volume I) ensures attention to the building of a classroom discourse community in the TL that develops over time.

The advantage of backward planning is that use of the TL and ways to promote comprehension and interaction can be anticipated, and even scripted, if necessary, based on teachers' knowledge of what learners know and can do, and not left to chance when students experience difficulty. Further, a focus on learning outcomes (at both the lesson and unit level) enables teachers to consider in advance how to help learners experience success in initiating, participating in, and sustaining interactions in the TL (see HLTP #2 in Volume I). Anticipation of student challenges and misconceptions is a high-leverage practice that has been identified in the literature for subject areas such as mathematics (Hlas & Hlas, 2012) and is an essential part of backward planning.

Deconstructing the Practice

The discussion of HLTP #7 in the previous chapter deconstructed how a context is established as the foundation for engaging in planning and framing the content of the lesson. As that discussion showed, it is critical that a meaningful context, including the inquiry question, not only be established at the *start* of instructional planning, but also be *carried through* assessments and learning experiences. A tool for backward-design planning for foreign language is illustrated in Figure 8.1. The steps in Stage 1 (Establish the Context) were deconstructed in the previous chapter and should be reviewed when using the tool. Stages 2, 3, 4, and 5, which follow the backward-design process, are deconstructed below.

As mentioned earlier, the backward-design approach as applied in other subject areas has been modified in this HLTP to address the unique features of foreign language planning. Unlike other disciplines, foreign language education entails not only learning of content but also development of language proficiency. Therefore, the practice (i.e., tool) as presented here accounts for the iterative nature of planning for foreign language instruction. A critical feature of this model is that the steps are *iterative*—work on one stage of the backward planning may necessitate a return to a previous stage to make changes in the plan. For example, in a study described earlier, Paesani (2017) noted the bi-directionality of parts of the backward design model, commenting specifically on how the determination of acceptable evidence can modify previous decisions made regarding instructional practices or the identification of learning objectives.

To this end, Figure 8.2 depicts the iterative nature of the backward-planning model visually to illustrate the possibility of repeated cycles of decision making for each step during the planning process. That is, while backward planning typically advances from Stage 1 to Stage 2, to Stage 3, to Stage 4, and finally to Stage 5, sometimes teachers may find it necessary to return to an earlier stage to make an adjustment, and these 'possible' re-iterations are visually depicted by means of the dotted arrows. For example, while planning learning experiences in Stage 4, a teacher may need to return to Stage 2 to change a desired outcome to account for the fact that learners may lack the language proficiency required by the original outcome (see the dotted arrow between Stage 4 and Stage 2). Figure 8.2 also depicts the process as beginning and ending with a meaningful and relevant inquiry question (as depicted at the top of the model) and the context in which the question will

Stage	Purpose	Steps/Questions to Consider
1 – Establish the Context (See HLTP #7)	What context will be the impetus for meaning making and communicative interaction?	1. Establish the topic of the lesson or unit. 2. Identify one inquiry question that drives the topic or theme. 3. Identify the language functions of the lesson/unit and how they relate to the context. 4. Identify the grammar and vocabulary relevant to the context.
2 – Identify Desired Outcomes	What will learners know and be able to do by the end of the lesson/unit?	1. Identify the desired learner-centered outcomes or objectives of the lesson or unit. 2. Identify the goal areas and standards from the *World-Readiness Standards for Learning Languages* addressed in the lesson or unit. 3. Reflect on learners' background knowledge and learning needs.
3 – Determine Acceptable Assessment Evidence	What evidence will show that learners have produced desired outcomes?	1. What is the best proof that learners have achieved the desired outcomes or objectives of the lesson or unit? 2. How can I assess performance within the context established in the earlier stages of planning? 3. What will I ask learners to do so that I obtain this evidence? 4. How will learners know whether they achieved the desired outcomes or objectives? 5. How will I provide feedback to learners?
4 – Plan Learning Experiences	What sequence of teaching and learning experiences will enable students to demonstrate the desired outcomes?	1. What type of input will I need to provide in the TL and how will I check for understanding? 2. What communicative interactions will occur and how will they reflect the context developed in an earlier stage of planning? 3. How do I know that the tasks and activities I design reflect the desired outcomes? 4. Do the learning activities have a purpose and are they meaningful to learners? 5. How can I sequence learning experiences to scaffold student success toward learning outcomes? 6. What resources will I need to design the lesson/unit (e.g., authentic texts, visuals, realia, technology)?
5 – Self-assess/ Reflect	To what degree were objectives achieved and how will the achievement of objectives (or lack of it) inform and improve my teaching practice?	1. Does the evidence confirm that the desired outcomes were attained? If the outcomes were not attained by the majority of learners, what could be a possible explanation? In this case, what will I do to inform my instructional practice so that learners can achieve these outcomes in the future? 2. Was the context carried through the learning experiences and assessments? 3. What components of the lesson/unit were most successful and why? Which were least successful and why? 4. What could I do differently the next time to make this lesson/ unit more effective? 5. What learning theories/frameworks supported the lesson/unit or could be reflected with revisions to instruction?

Figure 8.1. **Foreign Language Planning Tool: Iterative Process for Backward Design**
Source: Original material based on Wiggins & McTighe, 2005

Note: The stages are iterative in nature.

be explored. For example, in Cook and Quigley (2013), university students began the unit with the question of ways to ensure environmental protections on their campus and in the local community and ended their exploration of the issue in a final dialogic presentation on local environmental protection with community members, accompanied by visuals to support their findings.

In sum, Figures 8.1 and 8.2 illustrate the role of an iterative process for backward-design planning for foreign language instruction. This model maintains its focus on backward design in terms of first identifying an inquiry question, context, and desired outcomes, then determining acceptable evidence, and finally planning learning experiences. Planning begins and ends with the inquiry question, and a self-assessment/reflection stage completes the cycle. However, the model also accounts for the iterative nature of planning by allowing for a return to earlier stages of the process.

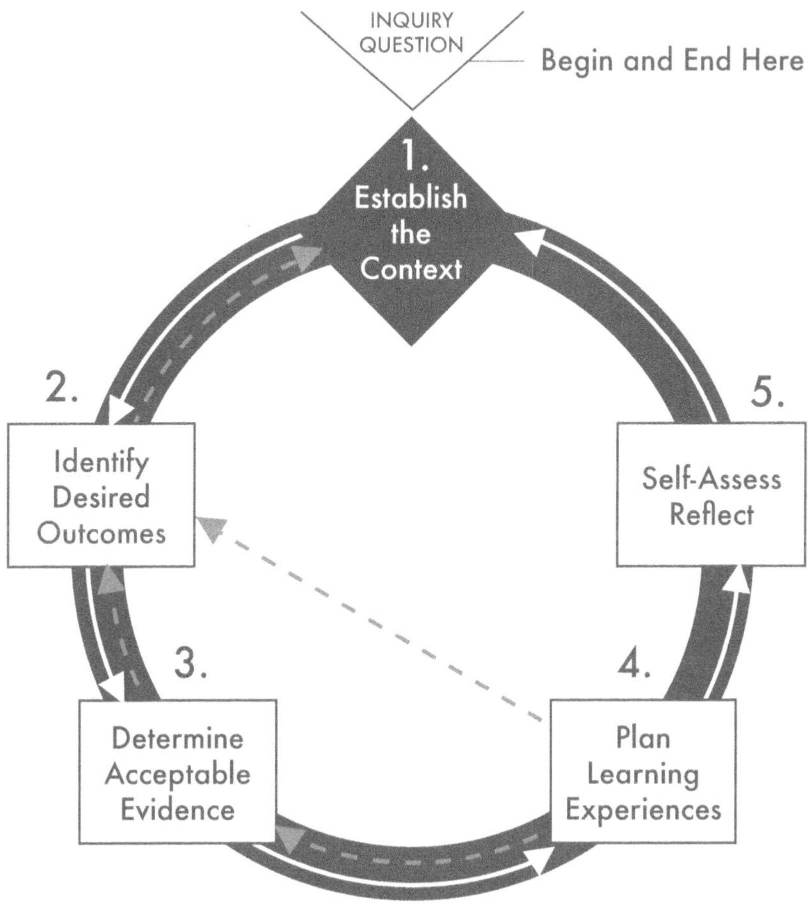

***Figure 8.2.* Foreign Language Planning Model: Iterative Process for Backward Design**
Source: Original material based on Wiggins & McTighe, 2005, and inspired by Windschitl, Thompson, Braaten, & Stroupe, 2012

Stage 1. Establish the Context: What context will be the impetus for meaning and communicative interaction?

The following are the steps involved in establishing the context, which were deconstructed in HLTP #7:

1. Establish the topic or theme of the lesson or unit.
2. Identify one inquiry question that drives the topic or theme.
3. Identify the language functions of the lesson/unit and how they relate to the context.
4. Identify the grammar and vocabulary relevant to the content and context.

Stage 2. Identify Desired Outcomes: What will learners know and be able to do by the end of the lesson/unit?

With the context and inquiry question established, the next stage is to describe the desired results in terms of the following steps:

1. Identify the desired learner-centered outcomes (i.e., objectives) of the lesson or unit. Objectives should be **functional**, and not based on grammatical structures alone. Functional objectives describe what learners should be able to *do* with the language in meaningful and communicative terms. As was seen in the previous chapter, grammar and vocabulary are important tools for enabling learners to attain the desired lesson and unit outcomes; however, grammar and vocabulary are not an end in and of themselves. For example, the following objectives have two very distinct foci. Only in the second case is the objective functional, that is, communicative and focused on meaningful use of the language.

(a) Learners will be able to conjugate the future tense. (grammatical focus)

(b) Learners will be able to discuss their future plans for after graduation. (communicative, meaning-based focus)

In addition to being focused on communicative use of language, objectives should be observable and employ action verbs that describe specific learner behaviors. Verbs such as "review," "learn," or "understand" are too broad and vague to describe specific, measurable behaviors. Similarly, using the word "vocabulary" in an objective tends to diminish the communicative nature of the objective; compare the following:

(a) Learners will be able to recite food vocabulary. (communicative purpose lacking)

(b) Learners will be able to identify foods that have high nutritional value. (communicative purpose clear)

Objectives should draw on the language functions that were listed in *Stage I: Establishing the Context.* All objectives need be stated in functional terms. One caveat is in order, however, and we might use the analogy of 'taking a trip' to explain it. Objectives describe the 'destination' of the lesson or unit—that is, where learners should 'end up', i.e., what they should be able to do by the end of instruction. The 'route' to the destination (that is, to the objectives) is represented by the various learning experiences—tasks, activities—that are designed in Stage 4. Hence, while lesson activities themselves support the achievement of functional objectives, they alone are not the desired outcome of the lesson or unit. The point of making this distinction is to caution against confusion of objectives and activities. For example, in HLTP #7, a culture-based inquiry question based on the theme of nutrition was provided: How do cultural norms influence our concept of good nutrition? One functional objective based on this question is 'To compare cross-cultural beliefs about what constitutes healthy eating habits.' This objective can be assessed by means of having students summarize the results of an oral interaction; it can be addressed in the lesson by means of classroom activities such as:

- Learners report back the results of a pair discussion about nutrition.
- Learners brainstorm a list of cross-cultural beliefs that undergird eating habits.
- Learners create a Venn diagram to compare eating habits between the native and target cultures.

Although these three activities will help learners reach the functional objective of comparing in the context of nutrition and culture, each activity does not represent its own objective as an end outcome in and of itself. For example, creating a Venn diagram is not the end outcome of the lesson but rather is one activity designed to mediate learning and assist students in attaining the functional objective.

2. Identify the goal areas and standards from the *World-Readiness Standards for Learning Languages* addressed in the lesson or unit. See Appendix 2-C for a list of the five goal areas and corresponding standards (National Standards Collaborative Board, 2015). In standards-based instruction at all levels, it is important to identify the standards that are being addressed in a lesson or unit, given that these represent expectations in the field of what students should be able to know and do as a result of language study. There are some important caveats to keep in mind, however. First, identification of standards is not simply an exercise in checking off boxes. There is evidence that novice teachers tend to list multiple standards in a lesson when, in fact, few are addressed in the learning experiences featured in the lesson (Donato, 2009). Second, there should be no expectation that all five goal areas must be addressed in one lesson, although this could be a realistic expectation for a unit that might last for several weeks. Third, teachers should strive to include a standard from at least one goal area in addition to Communication in daily lessons to avoid the habit of focusing exclusively on grammar and vocabulary without meaningful content in a clearly specified context for language use. Fourth, depending on the focus of the lesson, all three modes of communication (interpretive, interactional, presentational) might not be addressed. However, it is advisable to include interpersonal communication in practically every lesson so that learners are engaged in back-and-forth talk within a meaningful context. Finally, it should be noted that the two Cultures standards include the concept of cultural *perspectives* as a key element; therefore, addressing these standards means that products and practices must be connected to perspectives.

3. Reflect on learners' background knowledge and learning needs. An important part of planning is considering the learners. What pertinent background knowledge do they bring to this particular lesson or unit in terms of knowledge of the TL and of the instructional

context? What special learning needs must be addressed and, as a result, what adaptations need to be made? Would it be appropriate to differentiate instruction in the case of diverse types of background knowledge and learning needs? Perhaps some students have a higher proficiency level and/or have already acquired vocabulary that will be featured in the lesson/unit. In this case, some learning activities could be differentiated so that these students are engaged in more complex thinking. For example, learners in a class might be asked to identify names of foods that appear in a nutrition model such as a food pyramid. This activity could be differentiated for learners who have a higher proficiency level by asking them to compare the foods in the model to the foods they typically eat and then to evaluate their eating habits on a scale from healthy diet to change of diet needed. Complex thinking differs from the level of difficulty of a task, which only takes into account the amount of effort or time required to complete the task and does not consider the thought processes that must come into play. Hence, in the example above, asking learners to recall the foods that appear in the nutrition model (while not looking at it) would make the task more difficult but not increase its complexity. For more details about differentiation of instruction, see Shrum & Glisan, 2016, and Tomlinson & McTighe, 2006.

As learners' abilities and background knowledge are considered during planning, specifications for one stage may necessitate a change in other stages. As illustrated in Figure 8.2, work on Stage 2 might necessitate a return to the context to refine based on a consideration of the demands of the inquiry question. Changes to grammar and vocabulary may also be necessary to respond appropriately and adequately to revisions to the question in context.

Stage 3. Determine Acceptable Assessment Evidence: What evidence will show that learners have produced desired outcomes?

After the desired outcomes have been delineated in terms of learner objectives and the goal areas/standards addressed, and considerations about the learners have been made, valid and reliable assessments for providing evidence of meeting objectives can be developed. That is, what specific performance evidence in the lesson/unit will illustrate that the desired results (i.e., objectives or outcomes) have been attained? In this stage, assessment evidence is considered in terms of meeting objectives established in Stage 2 above, rather than primarily as an avenue for assigning grades.

The later chapter on assessment will illustrate that the most effective assessments are those that are seamlessly connected to instruction. This means that the context established at the start of a unit or series of lessons must be carried through not only classroom tasks and interactions but also assessments. Just as there is a danger of losing the context in the presentation of grammar and in the design of tasks and interactive activities, there is a similar challenge in designing assessments. When the context is lost, so is meaning, which often relegates assessment tasks to a purposeless manipulation of language forms. The next chapter will show that design of an assessment occurs in the planning stages of instruction (as opposed to happening after instruction is over) so that the context and goal of instruction are kept in focus. Further, context is critical in both **formative assessments** (those that occur throughout instruction while there are opportunities to improve learner performance) and **summative assessments** (those that occur after instruction is completed and determine what learners can do with the language at that point). Be sure to review assessments to verify that students must attend to the context and meaning in order to complete tasks.

The following questions can be helpful in considering the types of evidence:

1. What is the best proof that learners have achieved the desired outcomes or objectives of the lesson or unit?
2. How can I assess performance within the context established in the earlier stages of planning?
3. What will I ask learners to do so that I obtain this evidence?
4. How will learners know whether they have achieved the desired outcomes or objectives?
5. How will I provide feedback to learners?

For teachers who use a textbook and/or curriculum guide, the following questions might be helpful in determining the usefulness of existing assessments:

- Do the assessments contained in the textbook or curriculum guide integrate the context into all tasks that learners are asked to complete?
- Does the context play a pivotal role in assessments—i.e., do learners need to use the context to make meaning as they perform assessment tasks?

The practice of determining acceptable evidence requires performance on the assessment to demonstrate that the desired learning objectives have been attained. Both summative and formative assessments need to connect directly to the objectives, and both should be considered during planning.

a) *Planning and developing formative assessments*

The following examples of formative assessment strategies suggested by Clementi and Terrill elicit performance in each mode of communication while simultaneously checking for comprehension and understanding:

- Interpretive: Acting out the sequence of events or scene that is described; signaling—thumbs up/thumbs down, true/false;
- Interpersonal: Calling on a sampling of learners randomly to ask/answer a question related to the topic of the lesson;
- Presentational: Using a timed 'quick write' during the class associated with the topic (2013, p. 47).

Formative assessments are important for determining where students are still struggling, for deciding about adjustments to instruction, and for uncovering misconceptions that may lurk beneath the surface during whole-class instruction. For this reason, acceptable evidence means both ongoing assessment during instruction and summative assessment at the completion of units of study. Both types of assessments need to be planned so that instruction and assessment are seamless and the teacher is at the same time instructor, mediator, and observer of student accomplishments.

A type of daily formative assessment that puts closure to a daily lesson is the **ticket-out-the-door activity**. This activity is an effective way to assess whether the students can perform the objectives of the day's lesson while identifying areas that are still problematic, confusing to the students, or misunderstood. Ticket-out-the-door activities are also useful in providing feedback to teachers on the success of the day's lesson. The procedure is that all students must complete a short assessment task as an imaginary way to gain permission to leave the class. Examples of these ticket-out-the-door tasks might include asking students directly to explain the context and content of the day's lesson; inquiring which part of the lesson they thought was most important, most memorable, or still confusing; or providing a contextualized situation to which students provide a brief response. As the term suggests, these tickets should be completed by each student in writing or entered into a class website so that the teacher can review all responses, evaluate the day's lesson, and plan in an informed way for upcoming classes. This closure activity can also engage learners in self-assessment by asking them directly what performances they want to improve (see also the *NCSSFL-ACTFL Can-Do Statements* [ACTFL, 2013] as a way of engaging learners in self-assessment).

b) *Planning and developing summative assessments*

It is important to create the summative assessment during the long-term planning stage for a unit or course, so that it is clear what learners will be expected to do by the end of instruction to demonstrate attainment of the desired learning outcomes. While changes can always be made, an important step in backward planning is to determine the assessment(s) before planning classroom experiences. Examples of summative assessments are:

- An interpretive reading task in which students interpret a printed or digital text for the purpose of acquiring new information that will help them address the inquiry question;
- An oral interpersonal task in which pairs of students interact within the context and inquiry question of the unit of instruction, perhaps by engaging in a spontaneous role play of a situation or discussing a topic that addresses the inquiry question;
- A presentational task in which students create a product such as an infographic or student newspaper article that is situated within the context and provides information related to the inquiry question.

When the summative assessments that provide evidence of overall achievement are specified, classroom instruction and learning tasks can be more effectively aligned and student success can be supported. An additional advantage of establishing assessments before teaching a lesson or series of lessons is that expectations for performance can be made clear and explicit to learners, which can often motivate them, as explained earlier when discussing research findings on backward design. See HLTP #10 for a fuller treatment of how to design performance-based assessments.

Stage 4. Plan Learning Experiences: What sequence of teaching and learning experiences will enable students to demonstrate the desired outcomes?

In this stage, classroom experiences are planned in terms of what the teacher and learners will do in order to develop the skill and knowledge that will allow learners to meet the objectives. It is critical that classroom practice (i.e., interactions and tasks) maintain the context so that language use remains meaningful and purposeful. To this end, create activities that will enable students to develop functional proficiency in the target language within the context of instruction. Interactions and tasks should include a sufficient amount of contextual information (e.g., setting, participants, relationship of speakers, level of formality, tone, goal of the interaction) to make clear to students how the language makes meaning in the context of its use. If a textbook activity is selected in which the context is thin, it can be strengthened by adding additional features that render the talk-in-interaction meaningful, comprehensible, and memorable. Next, review these tasks to determine whether they will be interesting to students and if there is a purpose to the task beyond demonstrating mastery of grammatical forms. Any task whose only purpose is meaningless and mechanical manipulation of grammatical forms should be transformed so that it has an authentic purpose and concrete outcome. For example, imagine a textbook task that asks students to use the correct imperative forms in the context of completing a recipe from the target language culture, with no other purpose given. Several ways of creating purpose are possible. At the conclusion of the exercise, students could be asked to state whether they would enjoy trying the dish. A class poll could then be taken on who would enjoy the dish compared to those who did not find it appealing. Students could compare the recipe to a recipe they already know and make a cross-cultural comparison. Students could also convert the recipe to serve additional people and make the necessary modification to the quantity of ingredients using, for example, metric weights and measures. This activity could be changed to an information gap activity in which one person has some ingredients and the other has different ingredients and they need to determine a shopping list.

Keep in mind that creating or adapting a simple communicative task with a real purpose in context does *not* imply developing a fully formed class project that would require several days to complete. Purposes, when they are not part of the textbook tasks or activities, can be provided simply by asking students to use the information contained in the exercise in some way, such as stating an opinion or feeling or changing the information slightly based on a change of context (see discussion of field, tenor, and mode in the previous chapter). In this way, students go beyond only demonstrating that they can produce correct grammatical forms or lexical items and experience language use in context.

For teachers who use a textbook and/or curriculum guide, the following questions might be helpful in determining the usefulness of existing tasks and activities:

- Does the textbook or curriculum guide integrate the context into all instructional practices in the lesson (e.g., presentation of vocabulary and grammar, readings, cultural information, language tasks and activities for practice)?
- Is the context clearly present in the tasks and activities of the lesson/unit—i.e., does the context provide enough information so that students understand the nature of the interactions in which they will participate?

To this end, classroom experiences are developed and enacted with reference to other important high-leverage practices. For example, input must be comprehensible, student interactions with the teacher and with each other need to be framed in the context of the lesson to provide meaningful practice toward achieving the learning targets, and materials (e.g., developmentally appropriate authentic texts, visuals, technological tools, media) need to be selected to support instruction and interactive activities. The following guidelines can assist teachers in designing learning experiences:

- Develop communicative interactions and align them with the content and context of the lesson and unit developed in the earlier stage of planning (see HLTPs presented in Volume I to guide the development of learning experiences).
- Check that the learning experiences reflect and require use of the desired functional objectives.
- Check that the learning experiences have a purpose and are meaningful to students.
- Sequence the learning experiences across instruction, be it in a class or in a series of lessons, so that each learning experience builds on the previous one(s)—and always with attention to the outcomes (i.e., inquiry question). During planning, ensure that learning experiences are ordered in a way that scaffolds student success toward the specified learning outcomes.
- Check that resources that will be needed for the learning experiences are available (e.g., authentic texts, visuals, realia, technology).

Learning experiences are not only pair and group work tasks. Teacher presentations and interactions with the whole class are also part of the learning experience. During planning, also consider how teacher-fronted work with the whole class will be presented. As a summary of what has been presented in this chapter and in HLTP #7, consider the following factors (adapted from Shrum & Glisan, 2016, p. 97.):

- Conduct the most important parts of the lesson at the beginning of the lesson and at the end, given the primacy/recency effect described earlier;
- Introduce novelty and humor into the lesson;
- Begin the lesson in an engaging manner to pique the interest of learners;
- Alternate whole-class instruction/interaction with pair/group work to differentiate instruction and to provide various ways for learners to interact with the material;
- Close the lesson by checking for what was learned, remembered, or problematic, e.g., use the ticket-out-the-door activity presented earlier in this chapter.

The process of designing learning experiences that promote learners' ability to accomplish functional language objectives may reveal opportunities to expand or fine-tune those objectives and the assessments that will demonstrate their achievement. When this happens, the iterative nature of the backward-design process comes into play as the teacher reviews what was planned in the earlier stages, including assessments, evidence, and objectives, and makes appropriate adjustments.

Stage 5. Self-Assess/Reflect: To what degree were objectives achieved and how will the achievement of objectives (or lack of it) inform and improve my teaching practice?

After instruction is complete and student learning is assessed, the teacher should reflect on the results in order to determine to what degree the desired objectives were achieved and to inform future planning and instruction. Although this stage occurs after planning and instruction have been completed, it is considered a critical part of the planning cycle that brings the planning process full circle, from the initial identification of the inquiry question to a final reflection on whether learners were able to address the question because of the sequence of learning experiences and formative assessments in which they engaged. The following are sample questions that could be posed by the teacher to engage in self-reflection:

- Does the evidence confirm that the desired outcomes were attained? Were learners able to answer the inquiry question by synthesizing knowledge and skills that they acquired as a result of instruction and learning experiences? If the outcomes were not attained by the majority of learners, what could be a possible explanation? In this case, what will I do to inform my instructional practice so that learners can achieve these outcomes in the future?
- Was the context carried through all of the learning experiences and assessments?
- What components of the lesson/unit were most successful, and why? Which were least successful, and why?
- What could I do differently the next time to make this lesson/unit more effective?
- What learning theories/frameworks supported the lesson/unit or could be reflected with revisions to instruction?

Self-assessment and reflection bring the planning cycle full circle, inform planning done in Stages 1-4, and lead to improvement in planning and teaching for future lessons/units. In this way, planning, teaching, learning, assessing, and reflecting form a seamless connection that continues to be promoted in educational research as an effective way to have a positive impact on learning (see for example, Adair-Hauck, Glisan, & Troyan, 2013; Bachman & Palmer, 2010; Poehner, 2008.)

Rehearsing the Practice

The following tasks are provided to practice ways to engage in backward-design planning.

1. Which of the following statements would make the most effective functional objectives and why? For those statements that you determine are not effective objectives, how might you change them to make them functional objectives?

   a. Learners will learn about ways to make travel plans.

   b. Learners will be able to compare mealtime habits in L1 and L2 cultures.

   c. Learners will be able to design an infographic with tips for maintaining a healthy lifestyle.

   d. Learners will know and recite from memory the numbers 1-100.

   e. Learners will be able to list their daily activities on a typical school day.

   f. Learners will be able to understand how to form the present tense.

   g. Learners will be able to recommend an itinerary for a trip.

   h. Learners will be able to play a game to practice food vocabulary.

2. Choose one of the following contexts stated in terms of topics/inquiry questions. Then design five performance-based objectives (Stage 2: Identify Desired Outcomes) that could be included in a unit or series of lessons dealing with this context. Identify the goal areas and standards of the *World-Readiness Standards for Learning Languages* that correspond to these objectives (see Appendix 2-C). Finally, what grammar and vocabulary would be necessary to attain these objectives and standards?

- Topic: School; Inquiry Question: How does the educational system in a country shape the daily lives of young people?
- Topic: Leisure-time Activities: How does leisure time in France compare to leisure time in the United States?

3. For the previous task, design Stage 3: Determine Acceptable Assessment Evidence by answering the questions posed in the earlier discussion of this stage.

4. Return to Task #5 in the previous chapter, in which you designed the planning for Stage 1 involving establishing the context. Now design a daily lesson plan for this context by completing Stages 2, 3, and 4 of the framework. You may find it helpful to use External Mediational Tool #8 in Appendix 2-A. If possible, teach this lesson to students or a group of your peers.

Assessing the Practice

Use Rubric #8 in Appendix 2-B to self-assess the lesson you developed in (4) above. As an alternative or in addition, you could ask a colleague to review a lesson that you have planned (and/or observe it) and provide feedback using the appropriate categories on the rubric.

Putting the Practice into a Larger Context: Instructional Goals and Challenges

As was explored earlier in the chapter, novice teachers often struggle with the complex practice of instructional planning. To this end, published work on high-leverage practices has included planning as a critical practice central to student learning and effective teaching. In this regard, Teaching Works (2020) has identified the following HLTPs that deal with the planning process:

- #13. Setting long- and short-term learning goals for students
- #14. Designing single lessons and sequences of lessons
- #15. Checking student understanding during and at the conclusion of lessons
- #16. Selecting and designing formal assessments of student learning
- #17. Interpreting the results of student work, including routine assignments, quizzes, tests, projects, and standardized assessments
- #19. Analyzing instruction for the purpose of improving it

Effective planning has been identified as a high-leverage practice across disciplines such as English language learning (Chang, Lozano, Neri, & Herman, 2017), science (Windschitl, Thompson, Braaten, & Stroupe, 2012), and special education (McLeskey, 2017), to name only a few. Five common threads are deemed critical in HLTPs that deal with planning, regardless of the subject matter:

- Keeping end goals and objectives in mind when planning instruction;
- Activating students' background knowledge;
- Sequencing the lesson parts carefully and providing sufficient scaffolding to enhance understanding and learning;
- Assessing whether students have attained desired objectives; and
- Analyzing instruction to evaluate its effectiveness.

Backward planning represents a principled and systematic way of considering how to plan that is embraced across various academic disciplines at all levels of instruction. Designing instruction using a backward-design approach requires understanding that planning is not a linear process but one that is cyclical and iterative. Hence, this HLTP addresses the challenge involved in backward planning by depicting it as part of an iterative process. As stages in the planning process take shape and are defined, other stages may need to be reviewed and redesigned. Secondly, the bi-directional nature of the model reflects teacher cognition and how teachers actually conceptualize and engage in the planning process. Finally, backward planning puts students at the center by creating a map of the educational journey in advance of the trip, identifying destinations, describing routes, and finally deciding if the map actually brought the travelers to the desired destination.

References

Adair-Hauck, B., Glisan, E. W., & Troyan, F. J. (2013). *Implementing Integrated Performance Assessment.* Alexandria, VA: ACTFL.

American Council on the Teaching of Foreign Languages (ACTFL). (2010). ACTFL position statement on use of the target language in the classroom. Arlington, VA: Author. Retrieved from http://www.actfl.org/news/position-statements/use-the-target-language-the-classroom

American Council on the Teaching of Foreign Languages (ACTFL). (2012a). *ACTFL performance descriptors for language learners.* Alexandria, VA: Author. Retrieved from http://www.actfl.org/publications/guidelines-and-manuals/actfl-performance-descriptors-language-learners

American Council on the Teaching of Foreign Languages (ACTFL). (2012b). *ACTFL proficiency guidelines.* Alexandria, VA: Author. Retrieved from http://www.actfl.org/publications/guidelines-and-manuals/actfl-proficiency-guidelines-2012

American Council on the Teaching of Foreign Languages (ACTFL). (2013). *NCSSFL-ACTFL can-do statements.* Alexandria, VA: Author. Retrieved from http://www.actfl.org/publications/guidelines-and-manuals/ncssfl-actfl-can-do-statements

Andreasen, A. R. (1985). Backward market research. *Harvard Business Review*, *63*(3), 176-182.

Ausubel, D. P. (2012). *The acquisition and retention of knowledge: A cognitive view.* Springer Science & Business Media.

Bachman, L. F., & Palmer, A. (2010). *Language assessment in practice.* Oxford: Oxford University Press.

Byrnes, H., Maxim, H. H., & Norris, J. (2010). Realizing advanced foreign language writing development in collegiate education: Curricular design, pedagogy, assessment. *Modern Language Journal, 94(s1),* 1–235.

Chang, S., Lozano, M., Neri, R., & Herman, J. (2017). *High-leverage principles of effective instruction for English learners. From college and career ready standards to teaching and learning in the classroom: A series of resources for teachers.* Los Angeles, CA: The Regents of the University of California.

Clementi, D., & Terrill, L. (2013). *The keys to planning for learning.* Alexandria, VA: ACTFL.

Cook, K., & Quigley, C. F. (2013). Connecting to our community: Utilizing Photovoice as a pedagogical tool to connect science students to science. *International Journal of Environmental & Science Education, 8*(2), 339-357.

Cooper, K. M., Soneral, P. A. G., & Brownell, S. E. (2017). Define your goals before you design a CURE: A call to use backward design in planning course-based undergraduate research experiences. *Journal of Microbiology & Biology Education, 18*(2), 1-7. doi: 10.1128/jmbe.v18i2.1287

Council of Europe. (2001). *Common European Framework of Reference for Languages.* Cambridge: Cambridge University Press.

Curran, C. A. (1976). *Counseling-Learning in second languages.* Apple River, IL: Apple River Press.

Daugherty, K. K. (2006). Backward course design: Making the end the beginning. *American Journal of Pharmaceutical Education, 70*(6), Article 135.

Davidovitch, N. (2013). Learning-centered teaching and backward course design—From transferring knowledge to teaching skills. *Journal of International Education Research, 9*(4), 329-338. doi: 10.19030/jier.v9i4.8084

Deane, M., & O'Neill, P. (2011). *Writing in the disciplines.* London: Palgrave Macmillan.

Donato, R. (2009). Teacher education in the age of standards of professional practice. *Modern Language Journal, 93*(2), 267-270.

Fuglei, M. (September 2, 2015). *Begin at the end: How backwards design enriches lesson planning.* A blog by Concordia University-Portland. Retrieved from https://education.cu-portland.edu/blog/classroom-resources/backwards-design-lesson-planning/

Gattegno, C. (1972). *Teaching foreign languages in schools: The Silent Way* (2nd ed.). New York: Educational Solutions.

Gazzaniga, M. S., Ivry, R. B., & Mangun, G. R. (2002). *Cognitive neuroscience: The biology of the mind* (2nd ed.). New York: Norton.

Graff, N. (2011). "An effective and agonizing way to learn": Backwards design and new teachers' preparation for planning curriculum. *Teacher Education Quarterly 38*(3), 151-168.

Harpe, S. E., Phipps, L. B., & Alowayesh, M. S. (2012). Effects of a learning-centered approach to assessment on students' attitudes towards and knowledge of statistics. *Currents in Pharmacy Teaching and Learning, 4*, 247–255.

Herro, D. (2018). *A qualitative single case study on backward design lesson planning experiences of teachers in a professional learning community* (doctoral dissertation). Northcentral University, San Diego, CA.

Hlas, A. C., & Hlas, C. S. (2012). A review of high-leverage teaching practices: Making connections between mathematics and foreign languages. *Foreign Language Annals, 45,* s76-s97.

Hodaeian, M., & Biria, R. (2015). The effect of backward design on intermediate EFL learners' L2 reading comprehension: Focusing on learners' attitudes. *Journal of Applied Linguistics and Language Research, 2*(7), 80-93.

Jensen, J. J., Bailey, E. G., Kummer, T. A., & Weber, K. S. (2017). Using backward design in education research: A research methods essay. *Journal of Microbiology & Biology Education, 18*(3), 1-6. doi: 10.1128/jmbe.v18i3.1367

Jones, K. A., Jones, J., & Vermette, P. (2011). Six common lesson planning pitfalls—recommendations for novice educators. *Education, 131*(4), 845-864.

Jones, K. A., Vermette, P. J., & Jones, J. L. (2009). An integration of "backwards planning" unit design with the "two-step" lesson planning framework. *Education, 103*(2), 357-360.

Kauffman, D., Johnson, S. M., Kardos, S. M, Liu, E., & Peske, H. G. (2002). 'Lost at sea': New teachers' experiences with curriculum and assessment. *Teachers College Record, 104*(2), 273-300.

Kennedy, T. J. (2006). Language learning and its impact on the brain: Connecting language learning through the mind through content-based instruction. *Foreign Language Annals, 39,* 471-486.

Korotchenko, T. V., Matveenko, I. A., Strelnikova, A. B., & Phillips, C. (2015). Backward design method in foreign language curriculum development. *Procedia—Social and Behavioral Sciences, 215*(8), 213-217. doi: 10.1016/j.sbspro.2015.11.624

Lado, R. (1964). *Language teaching.* New York: McGraw-Hill.

Littlewood, W. (1981). *Communicative language teaching: An introduction.* New York: Cambridge University Press.

Maquire, E. A., Frith, C. D., & Morris, R. G. M. (1999). The functional neuroanatomy of comprehension and memory: The importance of prior knowledge. *Brain, 122,* 1839-1850. doi: 10.1093/brain/122.10.1839

McLeskey, J. (2017). *High-leverage practices in special education.* Arlington, VA: Council for Exceptional Children & Collaboration for Effective Educator Development, Accountability and Reform.

Michael, N. A., & Libarkin, J. C. (2016). Understanding by design: Mentored implementation of backward design methodology at the university level. *Bioscene: Journal of College Biology Teaching, 42*(2), 44-52.

Modern Language Association (MLA) Ad Hoc Committee on Foreign Languages. (2007). *Foreign languages and higher education: New structures for a changed world.* New York: Author.

Munby, J. (1978). *Communicative syllabus design.* Cambridge: Cambridge University Press.

National Standards Collaborative Board. (2015). *World-readiness standards for learning languages* (4th ed.). Alexandria, VA: Author.

Nunan, D. (1991). Communicative tasks and the language curriculum. *TESOL Quarterly, 25*(2), 279–295.

Paesani, K. (2017). Redesigning an introductory language program: A backward design approach. *L2Journal, 9*(1), 1-20.

Partnership for 21st Century Skills. (2011). *21st century skills map for world languages.* Washington, DC: Author.

Poehner, M. E. (2008). *Dynamic assessment: A Vygotskian approach to understanding and promoting second language development.* Berlin: Springer.

Polya, G. (1945). *How to solve it: A new aspect of mathematical method.* Princeton, NJ: Princeton University Press.

Richards, J. (2006). *Communicative language teaching today.* New York: Cambridge University Press.

Richards, J. C., (2013). Curriculum approaches in language teaching: Forward, central, and backward design. *RELC Journal, 44*(1), 5-33.

Sandrock, P. (2010). *The keys to assessing language performance.* Alexandria, VA: ACTFL.

Savignon, S. J. (1987). Communicative language teaching. *Theory into Practice, 26*(4), 235–242.

Sheu, D., & Chen, D. R. (2007). Backward design and cross-functional design management. *Computers and Industrial Engineering, 53*(1), 1-16.

Shrum, J. L., & Glisan, E. W. (2016). *Teacher's handbook: Contextualized language instruction* (5th ed.). Boston: Cengage Learning.

Shulman, L. S. (1986). Those who understand: Knowledge growth in teaching. *Educational Researcher, 15*(2), 4-14.

Sousa, D. A. (2011). *How the brain learns* (4th ed.). Thousand Oaks, CA: Corwin Press.

Stephane, M., Ince, N. F., Kuskowski, M., Leuthold, A., Tewfik, A. H., Nelson, K., McClannahan, K., Fletcher, C. R., & Tadipatri, V. A. (2010). Neural oscillations associated with the primacy and recent effects of verbal working memory. *Neuroscience Letters, 473,* 172-177. doi: 10.1016/j.neulet.2010.02.025

Stiggins, R. J. (2008). *An introduction to student-involved assessment for learning.* Upper Saddle River, NJ: Pearson/Merrill Prentice Hall.

Streveler, R. A., Smith, K. A., & Pilotte, M. (2012). Aligning course content, assessment, and delivery: Creating a context for outcome-based education. In K. Mohd Yusof, S. Mohammad, N. Ahmad Azli, M. Noor Hassan, A. Kosnin, & S. K. Syed Yusof (Eds.), *Outcome-based education and engineering curriculum: Evaluation, assessment and accreditation* (pp. 1-26). Hershey, PA: IGI Global.

Talley, N. B. (2014). Are you doing it backward—Improving information literacy using the AALL Principles and Standards for legal research competency, taxonomies, and backward design. *Law Library Journal, 106*(1).

TeachingWorks. (2020). *High-leverage practices.* Retrieved from http://www.teachingworks.org/work-of-teaching/high-leverage-practices

Terrell, T. D. (1982). The natural approach to teaching: An update. *Modern Language Journal, 66,* 121-132.

Tomlinson, C. A., & McTighe, J. (2006). *Integrating differentiated instruction & understanding by design.* Alexandria, VA: ASCD.

Tyler, R. (1949). *Basic principles of curriculum and instruction.* Chicago: University of Chicago Press.

Weierich, M. R., Wright, C. I., Negreira, A., Dickerson, B. C., & Barrett, L. F. (2010). Novelty as a dimension in the affective brain. *Neuroimage, 49*(3), 2871-2878.

Wiggins, G., & McTighe, J. (2005). *Understanding by design.* Alexandria, VA: ASCD.

Windschitl, M., Thompson, J., Braaten, M., & Stroupe, D. (2012). Proposing a core set of instructional practices and tools for teachers of science. *Science Education, 96,* 878-903. doi: 10.1002/sce.210

Appendix 2-A

External Mediational Tool #8:
Foreign Language Planning Tool: Iterative Process for Backward Design

Note: The stages are iterative in nature.

Stage	Purpose	Steps/Questions to Consider
1 – Establish the Context (See HLTP #7)	What context will be the impetus for meaning making and communicative interaction?	1. Establish the topic of the lesson or unit. 2. Identify one inquiry question that drives the topic or theme. 3. Identify the language functions of the lesson/unit and how they relate to the context. 4. Identify the grammar and vocabulary relevant to the context.
2 – Identify Desired Outcomes	What will learners know and be able to do by the end of the lesson/unit?	1. Identify the desired learner-centered outcomes or objectives of the lesson or unit. 2. Identify the goal areas and standards from the *World-Readiness Standards for Learning Languages* addressed in the lesson or unit. 3. Reflect on learners' background knowledge and learning needs.
3 – Determine Acceptable Assessment Evidence	What evidence will show that learners have produced desired outcomes?	1. What is the best proof that learners have achieved the desired outcomes or objectives of the lesson or unit? 2. How can I assess performance within the context established in the earlier stages of planning? 3. What will I ask learners to do so that I obtain this evidence? 4. How will learners know whether they achieved the desired outcomes or objectives? 5. How will I provide feedback to learners?
4 – Plan Learning Experiences	What sequence of teaching and learning experiences will enable students to demonstrate the desired outcomes?	1. What type of input will I need to provide in the TL and how will I check for understanding? 2. What communicative interactions will occur and how will they reflect the context developed in an earlier stage of planning? 3. How do I know that the tasks and activities I design reflect the desired outcomes? 4. Do the learning activities have a purpose and are they meaningful to learners? 5. How can I sequence learning experiences to scaffold student success toward learning outcomes? 6. What resources will I need to design the lesson/unit (e.g., authentic texts, visuals, realia, technology)?
5 – Self-assess/ Reflect	To what degree were objectives achieved and how will the achievement of objectives (or lack of it) inform and improve my teaching practice?	1. Does the evidence confirm that the desired outcomes were attained? If the outcomes were not attained by the majority of learners, what could be a possible explanation? In this case, what will I do to inform my instructional practice so that learners can achieve these outcomes in the future? 2. Was the context carried through the learning experiences and assessments? 3. What components of the lesson/unit were most successful and why? Which were least successful and why? 4. What could I do differently the next time to make this lesson/ unit more effective? 5. What learning theories/frameworks supported the lesson/unit or could be reflected with revisions to instruction?

Appendix 2-B

Rubric for HLTP #8:
Planning for Foreign Language Instruction: Iterative Process for Backward Design

Note: See Rubric for HLTP #7 for assessment of Stage 1, Establishing a Meaningful and Purposeful Context for Language Instruction

	Exceeds Expectations	Meets Expectations	Developing	Unacceptable
Stage 2: Desired Outcomes	All objectives are learner-centered, observable, and functional. Communicative interaction is the focus of objectives.	All objectives are learner-centered, observable, and functional. Majority of objectives are communicative.	Many objectives are learner-centered, observable, and functional. Some objectives may be communicative.	Objectives are lacking in terms of being learner-centered, observable, and/or functional, and/or objectives are not communicative.
Stage 2: Desired Outcomes/Goals & Standards	Effectively addresses at least one standard in more than two goal areas of the *World-Readiness Standards for Learning Languages.*	Effectively addresses at least one standard in two goal areas of the *World-Readiness Standards for Learning Languages.*	Effectively addresses at least one standard in the Communication Goal area of the *World-Readiness Standards for Learning Languages.*	Partially addresses at least one standard in the Communication Goal area of the *World-Readiness Standards for Learning Languages.*
Stage 2: Learners' Background Knowledge	Provides a detailed description of learners' background knowledge. Describes adaptations for special needs. Differentiation of instruction is at the center of planning.	Provides a description of learners' background knowledge. Describes adaptations for special needs. Includes several strategies for differentiation of instruction.	Provides a minimal description of learners' background knowledge. Describes at least one adaptation for special needs. Differentiation of instruction may be minimal.	Description of learners' background knowledge is lacking, and/or adaptions for special needs are lacking. Differentiation of instruction not apparent.
Stage 3: Presence of Context in Assessments	The inquiry question drives all formative and summative assessments.	Formative and summative assessments are designed to reflect the context.	Formative and summative assessments reflect some elements of the context.	Formative and summative assessments reflect elements of the context on a superficial level.
Stage 3: Acceptable Assessment Evidence	Assessments provide convincing evidence of meeting desired outcomes. Learners are engaged in self-reflection in an ongoing manner throughout the lesson or unit.	Assessments provide evidence of meeting desired outcomes. Learners are engaged in self-reflection at more than one point in the lesson or unit.	Assessments provide partial evidence of meeting desired outcomes. Learners may be engaged in self-reflection only at the end of the lesson or unit.	Connection between assessment evidence and desired outcomes is weak. Self-assessment by learners may be lacking.

Appendix 2-B (continued)

Rubric for HLTP #8:
Planning for Foreign Language Instruction: Iterative Process for Backward Design

Note: See Rubric for HLTP #7 for assessment of Stage 1, Establishing a Meaningful and Purposeful Context for Language Instruction

Stage 4: Presence of Context in Target Language Experiences and Interactions	The inquiry question drives all target language experiences and interactions.	Target language experiences and interactions occur within and are informed by the context.	Target language experiences and interactions have some connections to the context.	Context plays a superficial role in target language experiences and interactions.
Stage 4: Learning Experiences	Learning experiences are meaningful. Communicative interaction is the focus of learning. Learning experiences are sequenced to lead to desired outcomes. Novelty is key in the lesson or unit.	Learning experiences are meaningful and engage learners in communicative interaction. Learning experiences are sequenced to lead to desired outcomes. There may be some novelty in the lesson or unit.	Learning experiences are meaningful. Some evidence of communicative interaction. Learning experiences are sequenced to lead to most desired outcomes. No evidence of novelty in the lesson or unit.	Learning experiences are lacking in terms of being meaningful. Communicative interaction may be minimal. Connection between learning experiences and desired outcomes may be lacking. No evidence of novelty in the lesson or unit.
Stage 5: Self-Assessment/ Reflection	Thorough self-assessment of effectiveness of instruction, attainment of desired outcomes, and role of context. Offers specific, detailed suggestions for improvement. Links learning theories to practice in a creative manner.	Effective self-assessment of effectiveness of instruction, attainment of desired outcomes, and role of context. Offers multiple suggestions for improvement. Links learning theories to practice.	Self-assessment partially addresses effectiveness of instruction, attainment of desired outcomes, and role of context. May offer a few suggestions for improvement. Links learning theories to practice minimally.	Minimal self-assessment that addresses effectiveness of instruction but lacking in discussion of role of context and attainment of desired outcomes. Offers a few suggestions for improvement, and/or no discussion of learning theories.

Appendix 2-C

World-Readiness Standards for Learning Languages

Communication: Communicate effectively in more than one language in order to function in a variety of situations and for multiple purposes

Interpersonal Communication: Learners interact and negotiate meaning in spoken, signed, or written conversations to share information, reactions, feelings, and opinions.

Interpretive Communication: Learners understand, interpret, and analyze what is heard, read, or viewed on a variety of topics.

Presentational Communication: Learners present information, concepts, and ideas to inform, explain, persuade, and narrate on a variety of topics using appropriate media and adapting to various audiences of listeners, readers, or viewers.

Cultures: Interact with cultural competence and understanding

Relating Cultural Practices to Perspectives: Learners use the language to investigate, explain, and reflect on the relationship between the practices and perspectives of the cultures studied.

Relating Cultural Products to Perspectives: Learners use the language to investigate, explain, and reflect on the relationship between the products and perspectives of the cultures studied.

Connections: Connect with other disciplines and acquire information and diverse perspectives in order to use the language to function in academic and career-related situations

Making Connections: Learners build, reinforce, and expand their knowledge of other disciplines while using the language to develop critical thinking and to solve problems creatively.

Acquiring Information and Diverse Perspectives: Learners access and evaluate information and diverse perspectives that are available through the language and its cultures.

Comparisons: Develop insight into the nature of language and culture in order to interact with cultural competence

Language Comparisons: Learners use the language to investigate, explain, and reflect on the nature of language through comparisons of the language studied and their own.

Cultural Comparisons: Learners use the language to investigate, explain, and reflect on the concept of culture through comparisons of the cultures studied and their own.

Communities: Communicate and interact with cultural competence in order to participate in multilingual communities at home and around the world

School and Global Communities: Learners use the language both within and beyond the classroom to interact and collaborate in their community and the globalized world.

Lifelong Learning: Learners set goals and reflect on their progress in using languages for enjoyment, enrichment, and advancement.

Source: National Standards Collaborative Board. (2015). *World-readiness standards for learning languages (4th ed.).* Alexandria, VA: Author, p. 9.

Chapter 3

HLTP #9: Engaging Learners in Purposeful Written Communication

Developing presentational communication in written texts differs from developing speaking proficiency and requires its own set of pedagogical practices and place within the curriculum and program of study.

Many of the high-leverage practices presented in Volume I focus on oral communication within the interpersonal mode, given the prominent role of speaking in creating and sustaining social interactions. HLTP #3 dealt with the interpretive mode of communication in guiding learners to understand, interpret, and analyze authentic texts for the purpose of exploring and discussing engaging content, topics, and cultures. In this chapter, we address the high-leverage practice of developing students' proficiency in written presentational communication, critical for the development of foreign language literacy. Presentational communication, like interpersonal and interpretive communication, is used to achieve purposes and goals in a variety of social and cultural contexts. Within the Communication Goal area of the *World-Readiness Standards for Learning Languages*, the presentational standard states that students need to learn how to "present information, concepts, and ideas to inform, explain, persuade, and narrate on a variety of topics" ... [while] "adapting to various audiences of listeners, readers, or viewers" (National Standards Collaborative Board, 2015, p. 59). However, lurking beneath this global and rather benign statement of competence is the fact that each of the writing functions listed in the standard represents a complex array of textual features and discourse moves (Hyland, 2004; Swales, 2004) that occur in various forms of presentational communication. To explain, persuade, or narrate in speech is not constructed in the same way as writing a narrative about a significant event in one's life, writing a biographical account of a famous person from the target language culture, or composing a formal report on a laboratory task in a science class. For this reason, we maintain that explicitly teaching how written forms of presentational communication construct meaning is a high-leverage practice that all teachers need to understand and be able to carry out to support learners' development of written literacy.

Developing presentational communication in written texts differs from developing speaking proficiency and requires its own set of pedagogical practices and place within the curriculum and program of study. One reason why teaching learners to write needs to be addressed explicitly is that some teachers and students may incorrectly equate writing with the transcription of spoken language followed by error correction by the teacher. In fact, in many foreign language classes, written presentational communication is approached only in this way, with students simply composing what they say in written form with no conscious attention to how writing represents a different mode of communication with its own conventions and ways of representing information. When instruction about writing is provided, it often amounts to little more than brainstorming vocabulary and directing learners to use a particular grammatical form, and in some cases specifying the number of times the form needs to appear in the piece of writing. This practice may result in learners thinking that the purpose of writing in a foreign language class is only to display accurate grammatical forms and sentence structures, a perspective on writing that is also reinforced during corrective feedback focusing on error. Additionally, when teachers frame writing as grammar practice, either implicitly or explicitly, learners fail to consider that the contents and organization of their thoughts are equally important. It is, therefore, not surprising that in a recent meta-analysis of 25 years of studies of writing in foreign language classes conducted by Li and Vuono (2019), foreign language learners overwhelming preferred direct correction of grammar and vocabulary over teacher feedback on content and style. The important point is that writing texts in a foreign language requires more than knowledge of grammatical forms. Although control of the formal properties of language is necessary for writing, alone it is not sufficient. To learn to present ideas, concepts, and arguments in writing requires knowledge of the topic, conscious awareness of cultural writing conventions, and ways of organizing the text to fulfill specific social and cultural purposes—ideas that are explored in more detail below.

A second reason why explicitly teaching written communication is necessary is that many foreign language programs have evolved from a grammar-based curriculum to standards-driven and proficiency-oriented instruction focusing not only on what learners know but what they can do with the foreign language (Adair-Hauck, Glisan, & Troyan, 2013; Adair-Hauck, Glisan, Koda, Swender, & Sandrock, 2006). As Cutshall (2012) states, gone are the days when anyone would suggest that language could be taught on its own as only discrete grammar points. Exemplary foreign language programs today require students to be able to comprehend and write texts of various kinds in addition to developing speaking proficiency. For example, in content-based or content-enriched programs, learners need to be able to comprehend, interpret, and produce texts on a variety of academic topics. In programs that begin in the lower grades and extend to high school and beyond, students' ability to produce written communication becomes increasingly important as they move through the grades, whether in elementary and secondary school or in a sequence of foundational and upper-level courses at the university (Donato & Tucker, 2010). For this reason, learning to present information and ideas in writing needs to be addressed simultaneously with interpersonal and interpretive modes of communication from the beginning of instruction and should not be left to some undetermined time when it is thought that learners 'know enough language and are ready to write.'

A final reason for explicitly addressing the teaching of literacy in writing in a foreign language is that it is impossible for students to learn to make meaning in writing without school-based instruction. The complex ways that culturally constructed texts develop ideas in writing are invisible to students and cannot be learned intuitively from exposure to texts alone (Troyan, 2014). Without explicit instruction on how texts are organized, how language is used to express meaning in various social and multimodal contexts, and how written language differs from spoken language, students will not develop the ability to make meaning in writing, an ability that is necessary for progressing through a well-articulated sequence of instruction, engaging in critical thinking and problem-solving, and performing later professional work (Allen, 2018).

In this chapter, we introduce the high-leverage practice of teaching written presentational communication through a **genre-based approach**. A genre-based approach to writing involves providing learners with explicit instruction on the form and function of various kinds of written texts and the language choices involved for communicating to particular audiences. As will be discussed below, examples of genres typically taught in the curriculum include recounts, instructions, narratives, information reports, explanations, and arguments.
ACTFL/CAEP Standards addressed: #1c, #4a, #4b

Research and Theory Supporting the Practice

Re-conceptualizing Literacy and Literacy Instruction

Before summarizing some of the relevant research on the genre-based approach to teaching presentational writing in foreign language classes, the concept of **literacy** and its relationship to writing merits clarification. The concept of literacy has been (re)defined and expanded beyond the narrow characterization as only reading print and writing essays and now includes interpreting and producing multimodal forms of communication (Kern & Shultz, 2005). This expanded view of literacy and literacy instruction recognizes various technological resources for constructing meaning in digital form. As Kern and Shultz state, "The challenges of multiculturalism and multimodal forms of communication call for a revised definition of literacy that goes beyond...error-free prose as a measure of writing skills" (p. 382). Contemporary definitions of literacy encompass, for example, interpreting, producing, and evaluating textual information on the Internet and other digital media (Carillo, 2019). Nonetheless, this expanded view of presentational communication still depends on understanding language as a functional meaning-making resource for constructing purposeful texts in sociocultural contexts, be it a webpage, an infographic, a social media posting, or an academic essay. As Kern (2000) points out, to be literate in a foreign language requires the ability to create and interpret meaning through text, which entails an awareness of the relationships of genre conventions to their purposes and to their cultural contexts of use. Kern's definition of what it means to be a literate language user and writer makes clear that literacy involves much more than the ability to follow prescriptive rules for the production of grammatically correct sentences.

Genre Theory and Research on Genre-Based Instruction

A genre-based approach to writing instruction is not about teaching prescriptions for various genres or limiting the concept to the traditional literary genres of poetry, prose, drama, fiction, and non-fiction. Rather, **genre** needs to be understood and taught as "a process of construing meaning purposefully in writing" (Schleppegrell et al., 2014, p. 38) to achieve a goal in social and cultural contexts. For example, the purpose of a genre may be to provide directions or information, argue a position, tell a story, classify and describe, or evaluate a situation, character, or event. From this perspective, genre can be further defined as a staged, goal oriented social process. Staged, because it usually takes us more than one step to reach our goals; goal oriented because we feel frustrated if we don't accomplish the final steps; social because writers shape their texts for readers of particular kinds (Martin & Rose, 2008, p. 6).

Although several studies of genre-based instruction have been conducted in the context of subject-area teaching for English language learners (de Oliviera & Lan, 2014; Gebhard, Harman, & Seger, 2007; Ramos, 2015; Schleppegrell & Go, 2007), English language arts, and social studies (Achugar & Schleppegrell, 2005), relatively few studies in foreign language education at the elementary and secondary level have been conducted. At the university level, one notable exception is Byrnes' (2001) implementation of a longitudinal genre-based program in German as a foreign language at Georgetown University. This curricular innovation spanned four levels of the German program and had as its goal the development of advanced foreign language literacy in German as the learners moved through the four levels of instruction beginning at the elementary level. Findings from a longitudinal study of 14 students who participated in this program indicated that, by the end of the third level of instruction, students' writing had become more mature and academic, more syntactically complex, and more lexically sophisticated and dense (Byrnes, 2009). Additionally, Byrnes found that time was a factor and that the largest gains in writing occurred between the third and fourth level of instruction, indicating that "systemic interrelationships at all levels...had been nurtured along an idealized knowledge path" (2009, p. 64). Her study points to the fact that explicit attention to genre-based writing over time resulted in impressive gains in student meaning making and in advancing students' proficiency in presentational communication in writing.

The two studies presented below also support the use of a genre-based approach for the development of proficiency in the presentational mode of written communication. The studies focused on different foreign languages (Spanish and Arabic) and levels of instruction (middle school and university), but both followed a similar research methodology for assessing student outcomes after genre-based units of study. Additionally, by reviewing these two studies, an introduction to the procedures for implementing the high-leverage practice of genre-based pedagogy will be presented. For this reason, details of the genre-based intervention will be provided rather than a brief summary. What unites these research studies are the impressive improvements in student presentational communication in writing after the implementation of the genre-based approach.

In his study of a sixth-grade Spanish class, Troyan (2016) worked with a Spanish teacher to implement a genre-based lesson in the context of a unit on learning about historical monuments in Spain. The genre-based lesson explored the ways that historical monuments are presented and described in written texts. Troyan's genre-based lesson spanned five days and included student pre-instructional written descriptions of monuments followed by reading, discussion, and deconstruction of an authentic historical description of the famous castle of Alcázar de Segovia. In preparation for this lesson and his work with the teacher, Troyan analyzed the authentic text so that the teacher could deconstruct it and describe its organization to the class using student-friendly, comprehensible Spanish. Based on Troyan's analysis, the teacher discussed with the class the various stages of the monument text, the function of each stage, and the specific language that was used to describe this famous castle in Segovia. The stages of the monument description text that Troyan identified were *El Título* (The Title), *La Frase con Gancho* (The Hook Sentence), *Datos Históricos* (Historical Facts), *Datos Arquitectónicos* (Architectural Facts), and *Organiza Tu Visita* (Organize Your Visit) to provide information on tours and to entice the reader to visit this castle. After textual organization was discussed and presented, the teacher focused on specific language choices that the author used when composing the historical monument description. For example, students explored the use of adjective attributes for specifying unique features of the monument and additional informational facts about the castle (e.g., at the confluence of two rivers, with a moat, with spacious attics, for Juan II). Learners were prompted to reflect on the meanings and functions of the language used at various stages in the monument description rather than answering low-level comprehension questions or identifying grammatical forms and translating vocabulary.

Following the deconstruction and analysis of the authentic text, the teacher and learners co-constructed a written description of a well-known conservatory and botanical garden in the city. With the teacher, the learners brainstormed ideas for organizing the text and describing this monument, and their contributions were recorded on a chart. When appropriate, the teacher reformulated student language by combining several student ideas into one sentence or suggesting ways to clarify ideas. Troyan states that "over 3 days, the teacher systematically led the students in describing the conservatory, expanding the descriptions they had begun in the earlier lessons on attributes and circumstances" (2016, p. 326). The post-test, in the form of an independent writing assignment, was given at the end of the joint text construction part of the unit. The analysis of the post-test to pre-test essays demonstrates that explicit and systematic instruction in writing in a particular genre resulted in greater detail, improved coherence and cohesion, and greater attention to audience awareness in students' independent writing about historical monument descriptions.

In summary, the phases of Troyan's genre-based unit were 1) selection of a genre related to the unit and learning outcomes (writing informational texts on historical monuments); 2) deconstruction of the monument description text in term of its organization and language; 3) co-construction of a written text describing a well-known monument in the city with the class; and finally 4) independent text construction by the students to determine gains in their ability to describe historical monuments and their awareness of genre conventions. This sequence of genre-based instruction occurring across several days, referred to as the **Teaching-Learning Cycle** (Martin, 2009; Rose & Martin, 2012; Rothery, 1994), will be explained in more detail below.

In a similar study, Abdel-Malek (2019) implemented a genre-based approach over the course of several days to teach the written recount (a sequence of events) to an intermediate-level class of university students of Arabic as a foreign language. Her study followed the same procedures specified in the Teaching-Learning Cycle described above. In preparation for teaching the unit on recount, Abdel-Malek analyzed an authentic newspaper article recounting a typical day in the life of the King of Jordan. Based on this analysis, she identified how this cultural genre differed from recounts written from a western perspective in English. Unlike recounts in English, Arabic recounts include more evaluative language to describe and appraise events in the sequence, statements about the main character's feelings, and explicit judgments of the character's behavior. Additionally, Abdel-Malek analyzed and labeled the stages of text for the authentic Arabic recount (title, orientation, sequence of events) and the purpose of each stage (e.g., introduce main character, attract the reader, establish time frame, establish chronology). This preliminary analysis of Arabic recounts by the teacher was needed for making the genre explicit and transparent to the class during the unit.

A pre-test in the form of a recount writing task in Arabic was assigned to learners so that comparisons in the students' written recounts could be made after the genre-based lesson. The pre-test writing involved watching a silent video of a professor's daily activities (e.g., woke up, ate breakfast, left for work, ate lunch, went to the gym) followed by the prompt to write an article for the school newspaper featuring a day in the life of this imaginary and well-known professor on campus. In this way, the writing task was given a sociocultural purpose, content, audience, and mode of communication.

The lesson on writing recounts in Arabic that followed included discussion and analysis of an Arabic authentic text about the daily life of a student, its organization features, and the language used in each stage of the text, e.g., the use of 'doing verbs' to express sequential actions and 'sensing verbs' to express the main character's feelings, and the specific way that Arabic creates cohesion in the text by dropping the pronoun and using verb morphology. The use of evaluative language (e.g., delicious lunch, good friends, interesting class) was also identified to show how the text created tone, in this case a positive depiction of the student's daily life. Analysis was followed by the teacher's collaborative writing with the class of a similar text about the typical daily activities of a student studying abroad and her positive experiences (purpose) to be published in the school's newspaper (context for presentational mode of communication in writing) intended to be read by the school community (audience).

For the post-test, the learners revisited the topic of the pre-test prompt and, for the purpose of comparison, were asked to write their own recounts of the daily life of a university professor. Three students of differing ability were selected for analysis of five aspects in their pre- and post-writing samples: the stages, the content of each stage, the organization of each stage, features that established the cohesion in each stage, and the evaluative language used to express the tone. Analyses showed that, despite differences in the three students' knowledge and skills, each one demonstrated greater skill in conveying meaning in the recount genre. All three writers improved by including each stage of the recount, organizing information of the sequential events carefully, providing evaluations of the main character's actions, and using Arabic language resources for creating a cohesive text. What was striking in the findings of this study was that learners not only improved the writing of their recount texts across a variety of features but also that improvements in their grammatical accuracy were also noted.

In summary, these two studies indicate three important points about genre-based pedagogy as an HLTP. First, even though learners might have seen previous models and had exposure to monument descriptions and recounts, they did not have a thorough understanding of the written cultural conventions necessary for these genres. Developing learners' presentational communication in writing in a genre required explicit and systematic instruction using authentic cultural texts as models. Second, a genre-based approach does not neglect attending to the grammar of the foreign language. In these studies of genre-based pedagogy, findings revealed that learners improve their grammatical accuracy largely through observing, discussing, and using language in whole texts rather than in isolated and disconnected phrases and sentences. Finally, both studies emphasize the importance of teacher planning for a genre-based unit and lesson. Troyan and Abdel-Malek, as well as others who have implemented this approach, prepared the lesson by carefully selecting authentic texts, determining ways to describe the discourse moves in student-friendly language, and identifying the type of grammar and vocabulary resources needed for realizing the particular genre.

Considerations about Genre-Based Pedagogy

(1) *What genres should foreign language students learn?* As presented above, genre is any type of text that has a social and cultural purpose. For this reason, a vast array of genres exists. In the context of school, however, the prototypical genres that are studied are recounts, instructions, narratives, information reports, explanations, and arguments (Derewianka, 2009). These overarching categories of genre capture many purposeful and social uses of language, such as giving instructions for preparing a recipe or for leading a healthy life style, describing a typical school day in a recount, expressing opinions on a current issue by constructing an argument, narrating a compelling story about an important person in the students' lives, or sharing research findings about cultural products, practices, and perspectives. These six categories provide guidance for identifying what genre can be explicitly taught that supports and is related to a particular unit of study. As Schleppegrell states, "While ... each genre may have infinite manifestations and is always changing and evolving, it is *still useful* [emphasis added] to think about the properties of prototypical texts that are associated with schooling contexts" (2004, pp. 82-83).

(2) *What are the advantages of a genre-based approach to the teaching of presentational communication in writing compared to more traditional ways of dealing with writing?* The genre-based approach takes a holistic view of language learning that focuses on making meaning and achieving communicative purposes in whole texts rather than on grammatical accuracy in random decontextualized sentences. Because genre is taught through the use of whole authentic texts rather than isolated sentences, real uses of language for real audiences take precedence over textbook exercises and the teaching of discrete grammar points for producing accurate words, clauses, and sentences. Further, this approach goes beyond the teaching of writing as simply the process of brainstorming vocabulary, assigning a prompt, specifying a grammar point, and providing feedback. A genre-based approach to teaching written communication makes clear how texts are organized and how writing is a purposeful, social process where texts are constructed *with* and *for* others, as the two studies summarized above illustrated (Christie & Derewianka, 2008).

(3) *What do I need to know to implement a genre-based approach?* Given that genre-based pedagogy is relatively new to foreign language education in the United States, the answer to this question is important for implementing this practice with fidelity and success. Derewianka (2009) presents an excellent discussion of how a genre-based approach might be implemented in language classrooms. First, writing needs to be *taught* (and not just 'caught,' as some might say) as real purposeful language use embedded into larger units of contextualized study. For example, students can learn about the conventions of writing narratives as they summarize or re-create a story that they heard during a PACE lesson (see HLTP #4, Volume I) or be instructed on documenting and organizing in writing a summary of major points after a text-based discussion (see HLTP #3, Volume I).

Second, Schleppegrell (2004) maintains that a genre-based approach requires teachers to develop for themselves and their learners explicit ways of talking about the language of texts. In the Troyan study, the teacher described the various discourse moves in the historical monument text in student-friendly language (e.g., the hook, historical facts, an architectural detail). Rather than rely on structural grammatical terms such as 'paragraph,' 'sentence,' 'noun,' 'verb,' and 'adjective,' the teacher and learners shared ways of talking about the text's language that emphasized what role phrases and words played in it and how they were used in functional ways to present information. One way to achieve shared language about text is in collaboration with the class. Teachers and students can analyze various texts and decide upon what a text might be called, how one text differs from others, and how various parts of the text might be identified (Derewianka, 2009, p. 5). For example, rather than point out nouns and verbs and subjects and predicates, the teacher might ask:

- What can we call all the characters in this fairytale? What about *participants*?
- How can we talk about the verbs in this history text? Are they all the same? Can we say some verbs show what participants *do*, *think,* or *feel* or how some verbs *link* one idea to another?
- Can we think of a way to describe the first sentence of this movie review? Can we say the first sentence is a *hook* that attracts the reader or an *interesting fact* motivating us to want to read more?

In this way, teachers and learners share terminology about the function of language of the genre that can be called upon in future lessons on writing. Redefining ways of talking about the language of texts can be challenging and requires a new mindset. This idea will be further explored in the deconstruction section of this chapter, and opportunities to work with this concept will be given in the section on *Rehearsing the Practice*. By way of introduction, in many cases simply using common sense about what language does in a text, rather than how it is an example of a prescriptive grammatical rule, is a good way to begin to analyze texts for making explicit to students how language functions and makes meaning in them.

(4) *Is there a place for creativity in a genre-based approach?* Teaching the various discourse moves of a genre seems rather prescriptive and locks students into only one way to write. Creativity and critical thinking are not compromised in a genre-based approach. One way to think about genre-based lessons is to consider the genre-based lesson as a framework for the basic features of the genre that provides learners with the tools to make meaning and build knowledge. As with all learning in life, control of the basics is required before creativity. Artists master rendering before turning to more abstract creations, musicians learn fundamentals of music before jazz improvisations, and novice teachers practice instructional and classroom management routines before implementing more complex and nuanced practices. One reason why a genre-based approach can be considered a high-leverage practice is that it provides learners with the fundamentals of various types of texts, which in turn gives them a framework for using language creatively and interpreting it critically as they progress in their proficiency in the written presentational mode of communication. (See the last chapter

of this volume for a fuller discussion of developing adaptive expertise with respect to enacting HLTPs.)

(5) *What is the role of grammar in a genre-based lesson?* Although grammar plays a role in classroom communication, this does not mean that every learning experience or activity needs to be reduced to a lesson about a new grammatical structure. Students need opportunities to consolidate what they know and use this knowledge for expressing their thoughts, ideas, feelings, and opinions. Language instruction should consist of more than the 'grammar point of the day.' Students need sufficient occasions for experiencing grammar in action.

Three important points follow from this position. First, a genre-based lesson is the ideal time for students to see how language is used functionally in texts and to use their language resources to create meaning. Second, model texts used in a genre-based lesson should be accessible to learners and not contain a large quantity of unknown or complex grammatical structures that create confusion in learners and require lengthy grammar explanations on the part of the teacher. Third, in a genre-based lesson, grammar, at an appropriate level, is experienced in context and for its meaning-making potential, rather than only its form. In the Abdel-Malek (2019) study, one unanticipated finding was that students learned how coherence was marked with morphology on the verb in Arabic, a grammatical aspect of the language that is traditionally reserved for higher-level classes in textbooks and curriculum guides. Without a lengthy grammar explanation and by observing this form in action during the joint construction of the recount text, students were able to use the form during their own independent writing. When grammar is experienced in a meaningful context, students learn grammatical aspects of the language and can actively put them to use for their own communicative purposes.

Deconstructing the Practice

Developing and teaching a genre-based unit or lesson will be deconstructed in two phases. First, and critical to a successful genre-based lesson, is *planning the lesson* by selecting the genre in the context of the unit followed by an analysis of the model text (sometimes referred to as the mentor text) that will be used to introduce the genre. The second phase of this deconstruction is *unpacking how the lesson is to be taught,* which will be based on the Teaching and Learning Cycle (Martin, 2009; Martin & Rose, 2005; Rothery, 1994), introduced above in the research review and illustrated in Figure 3.1 below. It is also important to note that the term 'lesson' as it is used in this chapter is *not* to be equated with one class period. A lesson could take place over several class sessions depending on the learning outcome, the length of the class period, and the ages and proficiency levels of the learners, among other factors.

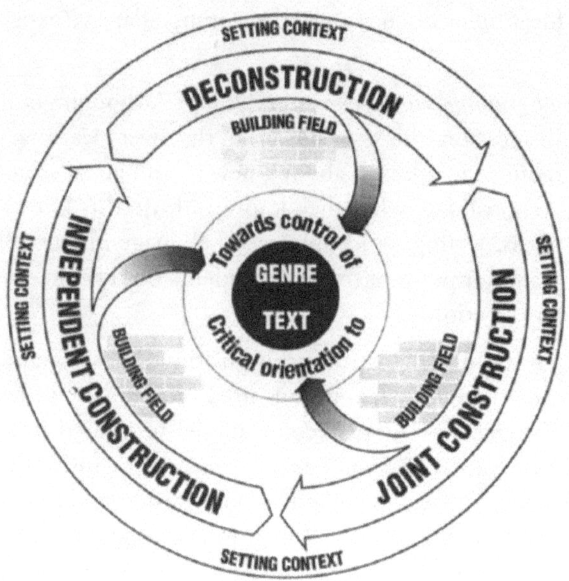

***Figure 3.1.* The Teaching and Learning Cycle for Mentoring Genre**
(Martin, 2009, p. 16) (Permission by RightsLink/Elsevier)

The genre-based lesson format presented in Figure 3.1 entails:

1. Setting the context and building knowledge of the field (i.e., knowledge of the topic);
2. Deconstructing the text with the class to identify textual features of the genre;
3. Jointly constructing a text of the same genre and on the topic with the class; and finally
4. Independent writing by the students.

Phase 1. Planning the Lesson: Selection and Analysis of Genre

1. <u>Identify the unit of study.</u> Select the unit in which the genre-based writing lesson will be embedded. Describe the context and content of the unit.

2. <u>Select the genre that fits the context and content of the unit.</u> Choose the genre that will be taught during the unit (e.g., explanation, recount, narrative). State how the genre is linked to the inquiry question and desired outcomes of the unit (refer to HLTP #8).

3. <u>Select an appropriate text that reflects the selected genre and fits the context and content of the unit.</u> Based on the unit of study, locate an authentic text that is relevant to the context and content of the unit, that features a genre relevant to the unit, that is interesting and well written, and about which students have some prior knowledge. The text selected should support the learning outcomes of the unit (see HLTP #8 on Planning), and the use of this text for the writing lesson should be integrated into the backward-planning process.

This text will be used for modeling and analyzing the genre with the class and, for this reason, the text should be short enough to present and discuss in one class period. Extracts from longer texts can also be used as model texts provided that care is taken in selecting parts of texts that exemplify the goal of the lesson and that can stand alone. For example, in a unit on healthy eating habits, writing an informational text might be the focus of the lesson in the form of a meal plan illustrating a particular diet, e.g., the Mediterranean Diet and a weekly listing of food choices for each meal of the day. In a lesson on cultural customs and practices, the narrative genre might be exemplified in a text or extract in which the author tells a story about a cultural holiday celebration with friends and family.

What is important in the planning phase is that text selection reflects the topic of the overall unit of study, that the genre will be useful for students when exploring the topic of the unit, and that students are familiar with the subject matter before introducing the text. This familiarity with the context and content is referred to as **field knowledge** (see Figure 1 above), a concept that was introduced in Chapter 1 on Establishing a Meaningful and Purposeful Context for Language Instruction (HLTP #7). Additionally, the text should be short, relatively comprehensible, and appropriate for the level of the class in terms of language and content so that the stages of the genre can be explored, discussed, and made visible in one class period. With longer texts, carrying out the steps of the lesson will take an excessive amount of time and, as a consequence, students will lose interest. If longer texts are selected for more advanced classes, the focus should be on a specific feature of the genre, such as use of connectors, types of descriptions, or choice of verb types and tenses. Another advantage of a short, comprehensible text is that the genre lesson can and should begin with reading and checking students' understanding of the text (see HLTP #3, Volume I).

4. Before teaching the lesson, analyze the text and identify the stages of the text, their functions, and the major language features of each stage. Although there may be variations in text structure even for a single genre, each text has a general and sometimes predictable organizational pattern that allows the text to fulfill its purpose in cultural contexts. Depending on the genre of the text, identify how it is organized into stages and decide on ways to label these stages in student-friendly target language. The stages of a text are the most predictable steps of its genre and are relatively easy to identify by asking the question, "What is being presented in this part of the text? – a description? an issue? a problem? an evaluation? a solution to a problem?" For example, narratives often contain three stages: an introduction (orientation) to the characters, setting, and timeframe, followed by a problem and concluding with a resolution and/or an important life lesson.

After identifying the stages, repeat the same process for naming the language functions in each stage and salient language features for realizing those functions. For example, in the Abdel-Malek (2019) study, the major stages of the Arabic recount were orientation and introduction of the main character followed by a sequence of events. Each of these stages had a particular function in the text by indicating who was involved, what actions took place, an evaluation of those actions, and where and when the events happened. The language features in the stages included, for example, temporal expressions (e.g., in the morning) and temporal clauses (e.g., after meeting with her students) to signal when events occurred in the sequence; evaluative language (e.g., exciting time, delicious breakfast) to establish the tone of the recount; and the use of 'doing verbs' (e.g., gets up, works) to express the daily actions of the main character and 'sensing/feeling verbs' (e.g., loves, enjoys) to express how the main character felt during the course of the day.

To summarize, Figure 3.2 presents a simplified example of the steps discussed in this section that a teacher would use to analyze a typical argument text that might subsequently be used in an advanced foreign language class.

Steps	**Examples**
Specify the genre	Argument
Identify and label the stages of the text	• Issue • Argument A, B, C • Conclusion
Identify the function of each stage	• Provide evidence • Convince • Persuade
Focus on the language features of the function(s)	• Language for expressing opinions and making claims • Verbs for reporting the words of others • Syntax for indirect discourse • Conjunctions and connectors for stating causes and effects

***Figure 3.2.* Analysis of the Argument Genre**
(based on Derewianka, 2009, pp 70-71)

A good starting point for identifying the language features of a genre, for example in a narrative text or as in the recount genre presented above, is to ask WH-questions. These WH-questions will identify who the participants are, what they do, see, say, know, and feel, and where and how they engage in these actions and experience these feelings. In this way, language is no longer an abstraction or an example of the application of a grammar rule but rather a tool for making meaning about the contents of the text and the writer's perspective on the topic. In addition to the use of WH-questions, texts can also be analyzed by identifying how the text is organized and the role and function of parts of the texts (i.e., stages) in the order in which they appear. For example, in an Information Report, the textual organization is often an opening statement of the topic of the report (e.g., The tea ceremony is a traditional cultural practice in Japan) followed by various facts about the topic that may be accompanied by illustrations, diagrams, and pictures. The function of the fact stages of the text is to provide details on each piece of information about the topic (e.g., The tea bowls used during the ceremony vary in age; some tea bowls may be over 400 years old.). As stated previously, everyday language can be used when identifying stages of a genre and the function of each stage. The terminology that we use to describe the genre of the model text should be comprehensible in the target language for the age and level of the learners.

5. <u>Finally, plan the timeframe for the lesson.</u> Will the lesson be taught in one class session or across several classes? For example, will reading and deconstruction require more than one class session, to give learners the needed guidance on identifying and labeling the stages? Will collaborative composition take place over two or more class sessions?

Phase 2. Teaching the Lesson: The Teaching-Learning Cycle

The goal of Phase 2 is to make visible the organizational features and language of the genre in anticipation of both a collective and an independent writing task. Before the genre-based lesson is taught, students would already be familiar with the topic of the unit of study through various classroom experiences, including teacher presentations and student tasks and activities specified during the backward-planning process. The steps in the lesson described below should be done, for the most part, in the target language and at a level that is comprehensible to the learners.

1. <u>Pre-writing: Present model text and establish its purpose and audience.</u> Share the model text to be used for writing instruction with learners using presentation software and/or hard copy. After reading and guiding learners through the text and checking their comprehension, ask them to hypothesize on the *purpose* of the text, where it might be found, and who might read the text (audience). For example, the text may be a short plot summary and review of a film that one might find on a streaming video site, or an informational report whose purpose is to provide facts to potential buyers about the features of a new model of cell phone, such as price and comparisons with earlier models.

2. <u>Pre-Writing: Deconstruct and explore the features of the text with the class.</u> After learners have read the text, identified its genre, and established its purpose(s) and intended audience, turn their attention to how the text is structured. Depending on the learning objective of the deconstruction, engage learners in exploring the various stages, functions, and language in the whole text, or focus attention on a particular stage and/or function of the genre, such as how characters in a narrative are introduced and the ways that language is used to describe them, or how opening statements are written in the introduction of an information report. These stages can be highlighted by the teacher because learners are often lost in a sea of words and not able to segment the text into its component parts or focus on a particular part of it. If using presentation software, highlight key parts of the text as a way of focusing student attention. This deconstruction step is similar to the Attention Phase of a PACE lesson (see HLTP #4, Volume I).

Deconstruction of the text should be carried out through interaction with the class in the target language and not as a lecture delivered by the teacher (review HLTP #4, Volume I, on co-constructing explanations in a PACE lesson). Learners can be guided to identify the various stages of the genre, their functions, and the important kinds of language used through the skillful use of teacher questions and suggestions. As parts of the text are presented, teachers may ask age- and level- appropriate questions in the target language to engage students in thinking about particular textual features and providing labels for the different stages. Having analyzed the text during instructional planning, the teacher will be prepared to offer terminology when responses are not forthcoming, to confirm student contributions, and to refine learners' understandings.

Sample Questions for Identifying the Genre:

- What is the main purpose of this text? Who might read this text and why?
- What name might we give to texts of this kind?
- This text is called a _________ (e.g., an information report). Why do you think this text has this name?
- How is this text different from other texts that we have read in class?

Sample Questions for Identifying Stages of the Genre:

- What is the writer trying to tell the reader in the opening paragraph? What might we call this section of the text?
- In this stage of the text, does the writer present a problem, a complication, or a solution?
- How many parts are there to this explanation/set of instructions and what name can we give to these parts?

Sample Questions for Identifying the Function of Each Stage:

- Where and when do the events of the recount/narrative happen and how does the writer tell the reader this information?
- What function does the introduction to the narrative play and what effect does it have on the reader?
- In this set of instructions, what does each stage of the text instruct the reader to do?

Sample Questions for Focusing on Language in Each Stage:

- What words does the writer use to describe and evaluate the main character? Is this language positive or negative?
- How does the writer tell the reader that the events of the text took place in the past?
- What types of verbs are used and what kind of processes do they represent (doing, thinking, saying, linking)? Why are these different types of verbs used in this text?
- Who is the participant in this stage of the text and what words does the writer use to describe her personality?
- How is the writer offering advice in the text? What words tell us that that the writer is giving suggestions?
- What word or words indicate that the writer is not certain of a statement that was made?
- What language does the writer use to make the main character interesting so that we want to learn more?

The sample questions above do not need to be asked in a linear fashion. Questioning during deconstruction requires some degree of flexibility depending on the focus of the lesson. The focus of the deconstruction phase of the lesson will depend on the model text, learners' familiarity with the genre, and the proficiency level of the class, among other considerations. How the deconstruction phase is carried out will depend largely on the learning objective of the lesson, which is ultimately to raise students' awareness of the purpose of texts, their organization (structure) for achieving the purpose, and the language used to construct meaning. Additionally, not every lesson needs to explore all parts of a text. In some cases, as was previously mentioned, it may be preferable to focus on only one aspect of text organization depending on the goals of instruction. That is, flexibility in presenting the analysis of the text with the class is possible as long as the analysis meets learning objectives and prepares learners for the kind of writing that they will do. The knowledge that learners gain from this phase of the lesson will, therefore, serve as the framework for writing carried out in the next two phases.

3. Writing: Collaboratively compose a short text of the same genre with the class. Collaborative writing of a text allows learners to reflect on and put into action the features of the chosen genre that were analyzed in the deconstruction phase. Additionally, teachers report that collaborative writing, when conducted dialogically, is the part of a genre-based lesson that learners tend to enjoy the most. Derewianka (2009) states that jointly constructed writing can be done by the whole class directed by the teacher, in a small group, or, if possible, between a teacher and an individual student during a writing conference. Like the deconstruction phase of the lesson, joint construction of a written text is interactive and involves scaffolding learners as they offer their suggestions on the content, organization, and language of the text and propose revisions. Additionally, jointly constructed writing guided by the teacher creates a class zone of proximal development (Vygotsky, 1986; Wertsch, 1984) where assisted performance by a more able person (i.e., the teacher or other members of the class) prepares the way for future independent performance, as will be seen in the next phase of the Teaching and Learning Cycle.

The joint construction phase of the genre-based lesson consists of (a) developing knowledge of the topic (building field in Figure 3.1); (b) establishing the audience; (c) discussing and recording with the class the information that will be needed to write the text; (d) eliciting suggestions and ideas from students by asking questions about features of the text; and (e) offering ideas, language, and possible revisions as the text is being jointly written. If working with the whole class, the text should be written on a large easel pad of paper or on a white board so that it is visible to all. The final text should be reproduced, distributed to the class, and reviewed. Publishing the finished product is an excellent way to make learners aware that writing in class is not just an academic exercise or just for the teacher but an act of communication to be shared with an audience. Several useful tools exist for electronically publishing students' writing (see https://edtechreview.in/trends-insights/insights/2900-great-tools-to-use-to-publish-student-work for useful internet tools for publishing student writing).

4. Writing: Engage learners in independent writing. At this point in the lesson, which can occur at a later time, learners are ready to engage in independent writing alone or with

another student. With the teacher's help, learners select related topics that are consistent with the topic of the unit. For example, in the Troyan (2016) study, learners read and deconstructed an informational text about a famous castle in Segovia. For their independent writing task, they were asked to apply their knowledge about the Informational genre and write about a famous landmark of their choice in their city. The purpose of this phase of the Teaching-Learning Cycle is to allow learners to put into practice features of the genre that they have learned, to develop control of the genre, and to work creatively with the topic. Although students will write using the general framework for the genre, independent writing is not to be confused with a simple reproduction of a model. During independent writing, learners express their own ideas using the framework of the genre as a writing guide. Critical and creative thinking about the topic should be encouraged as learners consult with the teacher during this phase of the genre-based lesson. Learners should also be encouraged to share their ideas for revisions to their texts and state reasons why a revision was made.

5. Post-Writing: Assess independent writing and provide feedback to learners. As with all performance-based tasks, feedback on and assessment of learners' writing need to be included to determine areas of writing strength and where more attention to the process is needed (see HLTP #10 in this volume).

Figure 3.3 is a tool for planning and teaching a genre-based presentational writing lesson in the context of a larger unit of study connected to desired student outcomes for the unit.

Rehearsing the Practice

The following tasks are provided to practice creating genre-based presentational writing tasks.

1. Select one of the genres listed in this chapter and find a short authentic text or extract of a text in the target language that is an example of this genre and appropriate for a class that you teach. For example, the text might be a movie review found on the internet, a news brief about a famous personality or event, an editorial on a current issue, or a brief informational report on a new scientific discovery. Using the genre analysis framework below, annotate the text in the margins, including the following four features:

- Identify the genre, its purpose, and intended audience.
- Select and give a name to the stages of the text.
- State the function (or functions) of the stages.
- Underline important language used for realizing these functions.

Share the text and your analysis with others in your class or professional development session to see if they agree with your analysis. You might find it helpful to refer to this chapter's External Mediational Tool #9A as you complete this task.

Tool for Planning and Teaching a Genre-Based Presentational Writing Lesson

Phase 1: Planning the Lesson

1. Identify the unit of study
State the unit of study in which the genre-based writing lesson will be embedded.
Describe briefly the context and content of the unit.

2. Select the genre
State the genre that will be taught during the unit (e.g., explanation, recount, narrative).
State how the genre is linked to the inquiry question and desired outcomes of the unit (see HLTP #8).

3. Select an authentic model text

Whole text or extract?	Genre?
Purpose?	Audience?
Cultural features?	Source?
Approximate length?	Level of difficulty?

4. Analyze the model text
How many *stages* of the text are there? (Most texts have relatively few stages). What can each stage be called?
What is/are the *function(s)* of each stage?
What *language features* are most prominent for each stage and function? Depending on the text type, language features should be few in number and related to the goal of lesson.
Do learners already know these features? If not, how will the language be presented?

5. Plan the timeframe for the lesson.
Will the lesson be taught in one class session or across several?

Phase 2: Teaching the Lesson

1. Pre-writing: Present model text and establish its purpose and audience
Ask learners to hypothesize on the *purpose* of the text, where it might be found, and who might read it (audience).

2. Pre-writing: Deconstruct and explore the features of the text with the class
State the focus of the deconstruction. Whole text? A feature of the text (e.g., stage or function)? Remember that a feature of the text is not just the grammar. If a grammatical point, state its connection to a function.

Depending on the focus of the lesson, prepare questions in advance that you will ask in the target language to focus student attention and engage learners' thinking about the model text and genre.

3. Writing: Collaboratively compose a short text of the same genre with the class
State the topic of the collaborative writing activity and how it is related to the model text.

State briefly how you will carry out this activity. What materials will you need?

Prepare questions in the target language that you will ask to guide the collaborative writing with the class.

Anticipate student challenges and possible ways to resolve difficulties.

4. Writing: Engage learners in independent writing
Prepare an independent writing task and state how it relates to the unit and genre.

5. Post-writing: Assess independent writing and provide feedback to learners
State how you will assess learners' independent writing (see HLTP #10).

***Figure 3.3.* Tool for Planning and Teaching a Genre-Based Presentational Writing Lesson**

2. Based on what you completed in #1, decide on how the name of the genre, purpose, audience, stages, and functions would be stated in the target language that you teach and at an appropriate level for your class. Refer to the Troyan (2016) study in the section on Research and Theory above for examples on labeling parts of the text in the target language.

3. Refer to a unit of work that you will teach and select a target language model text (or extract) that relates to the topic and that will be the basis for a genre-based writing lesson with the class. Share the text with your colleagues and explain how the text supports the topic and learning outcomes of the unit and how it will be used for a later collaborative and independent writing task. You might find it helpful to refer to this chapter's External Mediational Tool #9A as you complete this task.

4. Based on the analysis of the model text in #1, select a focus on one or more aspects of the model text and practice leading a deconstruction discussion with your class or members of your professional development group. In advance of the lesson and depending on your area of focus, write questions (in the target language, if possible) that you will ask to guide participants' attention on features of the genre that you have selected. The deconstruction discussion should be no longer that 15-20 minutes. You might find it helpful to refer to this chapter's External Mediational Tool #9B as you complete this task.

5. Practice collaboratively writing a short text during a mini-lesson with colleagues. The collaborative writing may be based on the model text you selected in the first activity. In this activity and depending on the type of writing you select (e.g., writing a recipe in the form of an explanation or composing an informational text on the rain forest), ask those to whom you are presenting to decide:

- The purpose of the text and intended audience.
- Important information that the text needs to include based on its purpose.
- The organization of the text (stages).
- The main language features that will be needed to write the text.

Based on the above discussion, lead the group in a collaborative writing task by asking guiding questions and giving suggestions, when appropriate and needed. For example, you may ask "How should we begin this piece of writing?" or "What information is the most important and needs to be presented first, second, and third?" or "What kind of words do we need here to describe the topic?" This rehearsal task should be conducted in the target language, if possible. You might find it helpful to refer to this chapter's External Mediational Tool #9B as you complete this task.

6. Students encounter a variety of academic genres in school that may create background knowledge and/or implicit understandings of how texts work. The purpose of this rehearsal task is to practice engaging students in exploring the general characteristics of how texts are organized and written. With a real class of students, select several short texts in your textbook or from other sources and ask students to scan the text and check comprehension. After establishing the meaning of the text, ask students to state (a) the purpose of the

text, (b) the way that the text differs from other texts they have read, and (c) any important language that they notice. Report back to your methods class or professional development group to describe how your students performed during the discussion and their ability to identify purpose, distinctive features of the genre, and specific language features that create meaning in the text. Based on your findings, decide on the area(s) of a genre-based writing lesson that you think will require the most attention.

Assessing the Practice

Use Rubric #9 in Appendix 3-B to self-assess the planning and teaching of a genre-based presentational writing lesson through the tasks you completed in #3, #4, and #5 above. As an alternative or in addition, you could ask a colleague to observe and assess a genre-based presentational writing lesson that you have created and provide feedback using the appropriate categories on the rubric.

Putting the Practice into a Larger Educational Context: Instructional Goals and Challenges

Learning to read and write the language of school presents a challenge for many students in all subject areas and across all years of instruction. Because some learners lack familiarity with academic language and because written language differs from their everyday talk, their ways of thinking and writing in school are often viewed as illogical, disorganized, and even as a cognitive deficit (Delpit, 1995; Lee, 2006; Valencia, 2012). As a result, Schleppegrell (2004) asserts, "In the absence of an explicit focus on the language [of texts], students from certain social class backgrounds continue to be privileged, and others to be disadvantaged…perpetuating the obvious inequalities that exist today" (p. 9). This observation has resulted in increased attention to helping *all* learners understand how written language construes different kinds of cultural meanings to support learners' critical thinking, academic success, and authority over writing. This ability is equally important in foreign language classes if learners are to progress beyond the most elementary levels of language proficiency. Additionally, the skills that learners develop in written forms of presentational communication in their foreign language class are potentially transferrable to other academic subject areas, as well.

Several studies, such as the two described in this chapter, have shown the power of making explicit to learners how texts work and how writers can control the language choices they make when writing texts. As Schleppegrell (2004) argues, "an individual's growth and development and ability to participate in society require…control over meaning-making in new contexts and…in particular ways…to develop interpretations, construct arguments, and critique theories" (p. 5). The goal of introducing the genre-based approach as a high-leverage practice in foreign language education classes is a way to give learners access, agency, and control over the language they write and read. For the profession, it is a way to connect to the theory, research and pedagogical practice already taking place in other subject areas and in many countries around the world. In this way, teachers move beyond the teaching of writing as a matter of translating oral language into a written form (Olson, 1977) or as merely an exercise for displaying students' command of grammar and vocabulary. Giving students the understanding of the way texts make meaning prepares them to participate in much more than a foreign language class. With this knowledge and ability, learners are better prepared for life beyond graduation; they will be able to assess critically the texts they encounter in the media and write texts that generate new understandings in clear and compelling ways.

Implementing a genre-based approach to writing is not without its challenges. First, and without denying the skill and dedication of teachers, it is perhaps fair to say that foreign language teachers are not fully prepared for unpacking and analyzing the complexities of written presentational communication in systematic ways that are informed by theory and research. Moreover, approaches to and assessments of writing tend to rely heavily on language issues (e.g., prompts, vocabulary and grammar brainstorming, error correction) rather than on purposeful text construction and content. To develop strong written literacy skills in learners requires making them aware of how various kinds of texts work and the language choices they can make to construe meaning in different social and cultural contexts of communication. But to achieve this teachers need to develop a new way of thinking about texts and the language that constructs them. What is critical is the ability to analyze relevant texts across a variety of text types and develop ways to engage students in exploring how texts fulfill well-defined purposes through their organization and language choices. It is also necessary to be able to identify and name for learners the various ways that texts are organized and function without reference to complicated linguistic terminology. This way of talking about texts develops and strengthens the classroom discourse community and anchors textual explorations in shared understandings about particular genres and the writing process.

A second challenge is understanding how to define a genre and its features. Common genres that exist in academic settings can serve as guides for teachers in developing lessons that support student growth in interpreting and producing presentational forms of communication. These school genres, however, are far from exhaustive and should not be understood as templates for writing formulaic texts. Genres are always evolving and changing as written texts are constructed to meet new purposes in new contexts. Additionally, many texts are hybrid forms and can represent several types of genre in a single text. For example, a narration may embed an informational text; Dora the Explorer is an excellent example of a hybridized text that combines informational and narrative genre in English and Spanish. The challenge is to make learners aware of the general features of school and everyday genres while not sending the message that to write means to follow a lock-step pattern of expressing ideas. Creativity, student agency, and critical thinking all play important parts in the meaning-making process in writing. Thus, genre-based lessons should not become a set of prescriptive rules for producing written texts. When learners engage in independent writing, they can be observed to improvise and modify for their purposes what was learned during the analysis of model texts. The important point is that students are given opportunities to present and justify the ways that they write and the language choices that they make about the contents of their writing.

This HLTP has an extensive research base and a long history of implementation in various parts of the world. It is time for the language teaching profession to address more directly the teaching of presentational communication in writing in informed and principled ways. As professionals, language teachers clearly know what they want foreign language learners to be able to do in their writing. The high-leverage practice advocated in this chapter provides a pathway to achieving this goal.

References

Abdel-Malek, M. (2019). Writing recounts of habitual events: Investigating a genre-based approach. *Foreign Language Annals, 52,* 373-387.

Achugar, M., & Schleppegrell, M. J. (2005). Beyond connectors: The construction of cause in history textbooks. *Linguistics and Education, 16,* 298-318.

Adair-Hauck, B., Glisan, E. W., Koda, K., Swender, E. B., & Sandrock, P. (2006). The integrated performance assessment (IPA): Connecting assessment to instruction and learning. *Foreign Language Annals, 39,* 359-382.

Adair-Hauck, B., Glisan, E. W., & Troyan, F. J. (2013). *Implementing Integrated Performance Assessment.* Alexandria, VA: ACTFL.

Allen, H. (2018). Redefining writing in the foreign language curriculum: Toward a design approach. *Foreign Language Annals, 51,* 513-532.

Byrnes, H. (2001). Reconsidering graduate students' education as teachers: 'It takes a department!' *Modern Language Journal, 85,* 512-530.

Byrnes, H. (2009). Emergent L2 German writing ability in a curricular context: A longitudinal study of grammatical metaphor. *Linguistics and Education, 20,* 50-66.

Carillo, E. C. (2019). *MLA guide to digital literacy.* New York: Modern Language Association.

Christie, F., & Derewianka, B. (2008). *School discourse.* New York: Continuum.

Cutshall, S. (2012). More than a decade of standards: Integrating 'Cultures' in your language instruction. *The Language Educator, April,* 32-37.

de Oliviera, L. C., & Lan, S.-W. (2014). Writing science in an upper elementary classroom: A genre-based approach to teaching English language learners. *Journal of Second Language Writing, 25,* 23-39.

Delpit, L. (1995). *Other people's children.* New York: The New Press.

Derewianka, B. (2009). *Exploring how texts work.* New South Wales, Australia: Primary English Teaching Association.

Donato, R., & Tucker, G. R. (2010). *A tale of two schools: Developing sustainable foreign language programs.* Clevedon, UK: Multilingual Matters.

Gebhard, M., Harman, R., & Seger, W. (2007). Reclaiming recess: Learning the language of persuasion. *Language Arts, 84,* 419-428.

Hyland, K. (2004). *Genre and second language writing.* Ann Arbor, MI: University of Michigan Press.

Kern, R. (2000). *Literacy and language teaching.* New York: Oxford University Press.

Kern, R., & Schultz, J. M. (2005) Beyond orality: Investigating literacy and the literary in second and foreign language instruction. *Modern Language Journal, 89,* 381-392.

Lee, C. D. (2006). 'Every good-bye ain't gone': Analyzing the cultural underpinnings of classroom talk. *International Journal of Qualitative Studies in Education, 19*(3), 305-327. doi: 10.1080/09518390600696729

Li, S., & Vuono, A. (2019). Twenty-five years of research on oral and written corrective feedback in *System*. *System, 84,* 93-109. doi: 10.1016/j.system.2019.05.006

Martin, J. R. (2009). Genre and language learning: A social semiotic perspective. *Linguistics and Education,* 20, 10–21.

Martin, J. R., & Rose, D. (2005). Designing literacy pedagogy: Scaffolding democracy in the classroom. In R. Hasan, C. Matthiessen, & J. Webster (Eds.), *Continuing discourse on language: A functional perspective* (pp 251-280). London: Equinox.

Martin, J. R., & Rose, D. (2008). *Genre relations: Mapping culture.* London: Equinox.

National Standards Collaborative Board. (2015). *World-readiness standards for learning languages* (4th ed.). Alexandria, VA: Author.

Olson, D. R. (1977). From utterance to text: The basis of language in speech and writing. *Harvard Education Review, 47*(3), 257-281.

Ramos, K. A. (2015). Using genre pedagogy to teach adolescent English learners to write academic persuasive essays. *Journal of Education, 195,* 19-35.

Rose, D., & Martin, J. R. (2012). *Learning to write, reading to learn.* Bristol, CT: Equinox.

Rothery, J. (1994). *Exploring literacy in school English (Write it right resources for literacy and learning).* Sydney: Metropolitan East Disadvantaged Schools Program.

Schleppegrell, M. J. (2004). *The language of schooling: A functional linguistics perspective.* Mahwah, NJ: Erlbaum.

Schleppegrell, M. J., & Go, A. L. (2007). Analyzing the writing of English learners: A functional approach. *Language Arts, 84,* 529-538.

Schleppegrell, M. J., Moore, J., Al-Adeimi, S., O'Hallaron, C. L., Palincsar, A. S., & Symons, C. (2014). Tackling a genre: Situating SFL genre pedagogy in a new context. In L. C. de Oliveira & J. Iddings (Eds.), *Genre pedagogy across the curriculum* (pp. 26-39). Bristol, CT: Equinox.

Swales, J. M. (2004). *Research genre: Exploration and application.* Cambridge: Cambridge University Press.

Troyan, F. J. (2014). Leveraging genre theory: A genre-based interactive model for the era of the Common Core State Standards. *Foreign Language Annals, 47,* 5–24. doi: 10.1111/flan.12068

Troyan, F. J. (2016). Learning to mean in Spanish writing: A case study of a genre-based pedagogy for standards-based writing instruction. *Foreign Language Annals, 49,* 317–335. doi: 10.1111/flan.12192

Valencia, R. R. (2012). *The evolution of deficit thinking: Educational thought and practice.* New York: RoutledgeFalmer.

Vygotsky, L. (1986). *Thought and language.* Cambridge, MA: MIT Press.

Wertsch, J. (1984). The zone of proximal development: Some conceptual issues. In B. Rogoff & J. Wertsch (Eds.), *Children's learning in the 'Zone of Proximal Development'* (pp. 7-18). San Francisco: Jossey-Bass.

Appendix 3-A-a

External Mediational Tool #9A: Planning and Teaching a Genre-Based Presentational Writing Lesson

Phase 1: Planning the Lesson

1. Identify the unit of study

State the unit of study in which the genre-based writing lesson will be embedded.
Describe briefly the context and content of the unit.

2. Select the genre

State the genre that will be taught during the unit (e.g., explanation, recount, narrative).
State how the genre is linked to the inquiry question and desired outcomes of the unit (see HLTP #8).

3. Select an authentic model text

Whole text or extract?	Genre?
Purpose?	Audience?
Cultural features?	Source?
Approximate length?	Level of difficulty?

4. Analyze the model text

How many *stages* of the text are there? (Most texts have relatively few stages). What can each stage be called?
What is/are the *function(s)* of each stage?
What *language features* are most prominent for each stage and function? Depending on the text type, language features should be few in number and related to the goal of lesson.
Do learners already know these features? If not, how will the language be presented?

5. Plan the timeframe for the lesson.

Will the lesson be taught in one class session or across several?

Appendix 3-A-b

External Mediational Tool #9B:
Planning and Teaching a Genre-Based Presentational Writing Lesson

Phase 2: Teaching the Lesson

1. Pre-writing: Present model text and establish its purpose and audience
Ask learners to hypothesize on the *purpose* of the text, where it might be found, and who might read it (audience).

2. Pre-writing: Deconstruct and explore the features of the text with the class
State the focus of the deconstruction. Whole text? A feature of the text (e.g., stage or function)? Remember that a feature of the text is not just the grammar. If a grammatical point, state its connection to a function.

Depending on the focus of the lesson, prepare questions in advance that you will ask in the target language to focus student attention and engage learners' thinking about the model text and genre.

3. Writing: Collaboratively compose a short text of the same genre with the class
State the topic of the collaborative writing activity and how it is related to the model text.

State briefly how you will carry out this activity. What materials will you need?

Prepare questions in the target language that you will ask to guide the collaborative writing with the class.

Anticipate student challenges and possible ways to resolve difficulties.

4. Writing: Engage learners in independent writing
Prepare an independent writing task and state how it relates to the unit and genre.

5. Post-writing: Assess independent writing and provide feedback to learners
State how you will assess learners' independent writing (see HLTP #10).

Appendix 3-B

Rubric for HLTP #9: Engaging Learners in Purposeful Written Communication Planning and Teaching a Genre-Based Presentational Writing Lesson

	Exceeds Expectations	Meets Expectations	Developing	Unacceptable
Genre Selection Within Unit of Study	Genre is linked to inquiry question and desired outcomes. Genre is embedded within the context and content of the unit.	Genre is linked to desired outcomes. Genre reflects the context and content of the unit.	Genre has a weak connection to desired outcomes but reflects either the context and/or the content of the unit.	Genre has a weak connection to desired outcomes as well as to the context and/or the content of the unit.
Text Selection	Text is engaging and builds upon prior knowledge of learners. Text features the context and content of the unit and embeds the genre.	Text is interesting and builds upon prior knowledge of learners. Text is relevant to the context and content of the unit as well as the genre.	Text is lacking in either interest level or connection to prior knowledge of learners. Text may lack relevance to either the context/ content of the unit or the genre.	Text is not interesting and lacks connection to prior knowledge of learners.
Analysis of Text in Planning Phase	Teacher provides a complete analysis of stages of text, functions of each stage, and language features using student-friendly language. Teacher provides additional details.	Teacher provides a complete analysis of stages of text, functions of each stage, and language features using student-friendly language.	Teacher provides partial analysis of stages of text, functions of each stage, and/or language features using student-friendly language.	Teacher provides incomplete analysis of stages of text, functions of each stage, and language features, with key details missing. Analysis may lack student-friendly language.
Deconstruction of Text with Class	Teacher engages learners in TL interaction in a creative manner to deconstruct text. Teacher asks appropriate questions to engage student thinking.	Teacher engages learners in dialogue in the TL to deconstruct text. Teacher asks appropriate questions to engage student thinking. Teacher offers guided assistance and confirms learner contributions.	Teacher deconstructs the text through a combination of lecture and dialogue with learners in the TL. Some English may be used. Teacher asks questions that do not always engage student thinking. Teacher provides limited guided assistance.	Teacher lectures to deconstruct the text. Dialogue with learners in the TL and guided assistance are lacking. English may be used.

Appendix 3-B (continued)

Rubric for HLTP #9:
Engaging Learners in Purposeful Written Communication
Planning and Teaching a Genre-Based Presentational Writing Lesson

Collaborative Writing of Text with Class	Teacher jointly constructs writing with learners as a whole class and/ or in groups. Joint construction is interactive and involves the teacher in scaffolding learners and offering suggestions. Final text is distributed to and reviewed by the class.	Teacher jointly constructs writing with learners as a whole class and/ or in groups. Joint construction is interactive and involves the teacher in scaffolding learners.	Students collaborate to jointly construct writing in groups. Teacher provides minimal scaffolding for learners.	Teacher constructs writing with minimal contributions by learners.
Development of Independent Writing Task	Learners select a topic and independently create a text representing the genre. Teacher encourages critical and creative thinking. Teacher provides helpful feedback on the genre features, including ways in which writing could be improved.	Learners select a topic and independently create a text representing the genre. Teacher encourages critical thinking. Teacher provides helpful feedback on the genre features.	Learners select a topic and independently create a text representing the genre. Learners mainly follow the exact model provided. Teacher provides feedback mainly on linguistic accuracy.	Learners are given a topic and independently create a text representing the genre. Learners follow the exact model provided. Feedback may consist primarily of a grade on the written product.

Chapter 4

HLTP #10: Developing Contextualized Performance Assessments

The teacher works with learners before, during, and after instruction as an ally to identify their areas of strength and to provide feedback that will enable them to progress. In this way, planning, instruction, and assessment are interwoven in a 'seamless' manner.

Historically, the term **assessment** has been used in educational circles, including foreign language education, to refer to something that was done *to* learners *after* instruction had taken place and for the primary purpose of assigning grades. Within this paradigm, assessments were typically designed at the conclusion of a unit of instruction, and in many cases, they lacked a meaningful context (see HLTP #7) and focused on discrete grammatical structures and vocabulary. Further, because assessment was viewed as being separate from instruction, assessments were not always aligned with the content and skills that students had learned, nor did they involve learners in self-assessment, i.e., documenting their own growth. Consequently, assessment results could seldom be used reliably to describe student progress or to inform instruction.

In recent years, however, the concept of assessment has evolved so that it is now considered an integral part of instruction and something that is done *with* learners *before and during* instruction. Indeed, the term 'assessment' has been traced back to its Latin root *assidere*, which means 'to sit with,' as in 'sitting with the learner' to determine what the learner knows and can do (Wiggins, 1993, p. 14). Accordingly, the role of the 'assessor' (i.e., the person who sits with the learner) is akin to that of a caregiver, manager, or coach, inasmuch as that individual displays respect and support for the learner, in comparison to an assessor whose function is simply to administer a test as a disinterested party. The current understanding of 'assessor' is a teacher who works with learners before, during, and after instruction as an ally to identify their areas of strength and to provide feedback that will enable them to progress. In this way, planning, instruction, and assessment are interwoven in a 'seamless' manner.

Educational assessment can serve a variety of purposes beyond that of assigning grades, such as discovering what learners already know and bring to a new learning situation, determining what learners know and are able to do as a result of instruction, comparing the achievement of individual learners to one another within a class, and charting the achievement of learners over time (Shrum & Glisan, 2016). Further, assessments can hold much power because they are used by assessors and stakeholders to make decisions about the future of learners (e.g., acceptance into a program, potential for future language study), language programs, or even language policy (Shohamy, 2001, 2006).

The first two HLTPs in this volume established the central role of assessment in the backward-design planning process. As illustrated in HLTP #7, the meaningful context that is identified as a first step in the planning process is carried through not only instruction but also performance assessments to ensure that learner progress is checked in terms of meaningful interaction, responses to the inquiry question, and attainment of functional lesson/unit objectives. In backward-design planning, as presented in HLTP #8, the teacher plans assessments once the context and desired outcomes are identified to answer the inquiry question, What evidence will show that learners have produced the desired outcomes? Assessments are specified before classroom instruction is planned so that instruction and learning tasks can be effectively aligned and student success can be supported. In addition, expectations for performance can be made explicit to learners, which can support the teacher in the role of ally and coach and can often motivate learners to succeed. As it pertains to assessment, the Iterative Process for Backward-Design Planning Model presented in Chapter 2 ends with the inquiry question that was identified at the start of planning, by assessing the degree to which learners are able to address the scope of the question by means of thoughtful responses or interactions in the target language.

In an approach to instruction that focuses on communicative interaction within a meaningful context (see Volume I and the other HLTPs in this volume), classroom-based performance assessments ask students to use the target language for communicative purposes such as exchanging opinions, presenting ideas in speech or writing to a specific audience, or sharing new information gleaned from an authentic text or a website. In his rationale for how language educators currently use L2 assessment, Purpura states that "we are specifically interested in eliciting evidence of L2 performance under certain conditions so that we can make claims about what L2 learners or users know, what L2 skills they have, and the extent to which they can use L2 resources...to communicate effectively within or across contexts" (2016, p. 192). Performance assessments motivate learners to show what they know and can do, unlike more traditional assessments that focus on recall of grammatical structures and vocabulary in a contextual vacuum. In view of the seamless connection of planning, assessment, and instruction, as well as the current emphasis on meaningful interaction, a high-leverage teaching practice for language teachers is *developing contextualized performance assessments.* Given the large grain size of this HLTP, this chapter focuses on three smaller-grain-size practices that teachers should know how to enact:

1. Creating and administering oral interpersonal performance assessments;
2. Creating presentational writing assessments; and
3. Providing feedback to learners through performance assessment rubrics.

An important caveat is in order. There are many kinds of assessments and assessment formats that language teachers could create and administer as part of their instructional approaches. The two types of assessments presented here are formats that would be part of a larger repertoire of assessment practices. Additionally, they were selected in part because of their relationship to the other HLTPs. That is, this HLTP is closely linked to the earlier practices presented in this volume as well as those practices featured in the first volume. In this vein, assessments are couched in meaningful contexts, elicit target language performances by learners, and reflect the instructional experiences in which learners have engaged.

ACTFL/CAEP Standards addressed: #5a, #5b, #5c

Research and Theory Supporting the Practice

The current view of assessment in education hearkens back to the claim made by Wiggins more than 25 years ago that "...assessment should *improve* performance, not just *audit* it" (1993, p. 11, original emphasis). In this regard, the focus of research in foreign language assessment over the past decade has been on connecting instruction and assessment, with the goal of using assessment to improve learner performance and inform instructional practices (Bachman, 2007; McNamara, 2001; Poehner & Lantolf, 2003).

As mentioned earlier, there is much discussion in the field regarding a 'seamless connection' between instruction and assessment, which can be realized in several ways. According to Bachman and Palmer (2010), assessment can take place in an **implicit mode**, also referred to as **informal assessment**, in which assessment occurs continuously and often without learners' awareness. For example, teachers may decide to provide oral corrective feedback (see HLTP #6 in Volume I) during oral exchanges to call learners' attention to a misunderstanding caused by a language error. Additionally, teachers may interact with learners to facilitate target language comprehensibility (see HLTP #1 in Volume I); through that interaction they assess the degree to which learners are comprehending and provide scaffolding to assist comprehension. Further, teachers may monitor learners' interactions in pair and group tasks to assess progress in relation to learners' current zone of proximal development (see HLTP #2 in Volume I). Assessment in the implicit mode is often labeled **formative** because it is used to make 'formative' decisions as instruction is under way, such as changing instructional strategies, providing additional modeling, and providing further assistance to individual learners (Bachman & Palmer, 2010).

Assessment can also occur in an **explicit mode**, also referred to as **formal assessment**, in which a task or activity is administered for purposes of assessing learner progress and learners are aware of it (Bachman & Palmer, 2010). These assessment tasks are connected to instruction if 1) they reflect the types of performance tasks and activities that learners have experienced in the classroom (e.g., students perform a spontaneous role play as an assessment, based on role plays they have done before in class), 2) they are followed by descriptive feedback to learners so that they know how to improve their performance, and 3) their results are used to inform and improve teaching (e.g., the teacher makes a change to instruction to improve learner performance). Assessments that occur in the explicit mode may be formative in nature, as explained above, or **summative**, in which they are administered at the end of a unit of instruction or a course to make 'summative' decisions such as whether or not students pass, what grade they earn, and whether or not they are ready for the next phase of instruction or course.

Empirical evidence has revealed the benefits of designing assessments that are intertwined with instruction. For example, a body of research has been conducted on the ACTFL Integrated Performance Assessment (IPA), a three-phase standards-based performance assessment that integrates the three modes of communication (interpretive, interpersonal, and presentational) and is intertwined with planning, instruction, and the providing of feedback (Adair-Hauck, Glisan, & Troyan, 2013). This type of assessment has been found to have a **washback effect** on instruction, by providing an impetus for teachers to change their classroom practices to strengthen their learners' performance (Adair-Hauck, Glisan, Koda, Swender, & Sandrock, 2006; Kissau & Adams, 2016; Shohamy, Donitsa-Schmidt, & Ferman, 1996). In the Adair-Hauck et al. study, 83% of teachers reported that implementing this type of assessment had a positive effect on their teaching, and 91% indicated that it had a positive impact on their design of future assessments. Moreover, it served as a "consciousness-raising technique" regarding their own teaching—e.g., they realized the need to integrate more open-ended speaking tasks and standards-based rubrics in their teaching (Adair-Hauck et al., 2006, p. 373). In all studies on this type of assessment regardless of the instructional level, teachers began "thinking like assessors" by contemplating the specific results they expected students to achieve before instruction was planned (Wiggins & McTighe, 2005, p. 150).

Beyond a washback effect on instruction, assessments that connect to instruction have been received positively by learners across levels of instruction. Research on student perceptions about learning has revealed that the way in which students perceive assessment has considerable positive and/or negative effects on their approaches to learning and, in turn, on their academic success (Struyven, Dochy, & Janssens, 2005). In her study of integrated performance assessment at the university level, Zapata (2016) found that learners were able to recognize the connection between their classroom experiences and what they were asked to do on the performance assessment—i.e., classroom activities prepared them for the assessment. Another study of this type of assessment with college-level learners revealed that the assessment had a significant positive effect on learners' motivation for and perceptions about language learning and their attitudes about an integrated type of assessment that is woven into instruction (Glisan, Uribe, & Adair-Hauck, 2007). Similar results emerged from a study of integrated performance assessment with elementary school learners of Spanish. In survey responses, learners indicated an awareness of what they needed to know and be able to do to use Spanish in purposeful and meaningful ways, and further, they articulated the type of instruction that would enable them to become more proficient (Davin, Troyan, Donato, & Hellman, 2011). The authors concluded that comments by students revealed that even younger learners understood the close alignment between the thematic unit and the assessment as well as "the seamlessness of teaching, learning, and assessment" (Davin et al., 2011, p. 617).

Performance-based Assessments

As mentioned at the start of this chapter, the concept of assessment in foreign language education has evolved over the past several decades. In the early 1980s, as a result of the *ACTFL Proficiency Guidelines* and the Oral Proficiency Interview, foreign language instruction underwent a shift from *what* was taught (e.g., grammar, vocabulary, textbook content) to what *outcomes* learners could accomplish (e.g., how they could communicate in the language) (ACTFL, 2012). As classroom instruction changed to become more performance-based and centered on proficiency goals, changes to assessment practices lagged (Troyan, 2012). Anecdotally speaking, it was common for classroom experiences to include meaningful communication and interactive speaking, while assessments remained traditional in nature (e.g., paper-and-pencil tests focused on grammar and vocabulary). Beginning in the 1990s, the focus on language performance in the classroom was expanded even further to include real-world competence in the goal areas of Communication, Cultures, Connections, Comparisons, and Communities, as a result of the national *Standards for Foreign Language Learning in the 21st Century* (National Standards in Foreign Language Education Project, 1996, 1999, 2006).

Performance-based assessments were born out of the need to assess students' ability to perform **authentic tasks**—those that mirror the tasks and challenges encountered by people in the world outside of the classroom—as well as those tasks that demonstrate their advancement on the proficiency scale. As a result, assessments slowly began to catch up with evolving classroom practices and to connect to instruction. In performance-based assessments, learners use their repertoire of knowledge and skills to interact or create a product, either alone or in collaboration with others (Liskin-Gasparro, 1996). These assessments require the use of knowledge and skills acquired over time rather than the use of a specific grammatical structure or set of vocabulary items. The format typically uses prompts or a situation in which the learner draws upon the knowledge and skills necessary for addressing the question or situation, through any of the three modes of communication (interpretive listening/reading/viewing, interpersonal speaking/writing, presentational speaking/writing) or a combination thereof.

Research on performance-based assessments has revealed positive perceptions by learners. In the Zapata study described earlier, university-level learners cited as beneficial aspects of the performance assessment "(1) the fact that they were now required to understand and produce the target language, instead of memorizing and using isolated decontextualized vocabulary items or grammar points in discrete-point exercises; and (2) the more authentic nature of the assessment, as learners felt that they needed to complete tasks that involved their use of the target language in communicative contexts similar to those they would encounter outside of the classroom" (2016, p. 98). Among the results of the Davin et al. study (2011) mentioned above, elementary school learners reported that the performance assessment enabled them to show what they knew (as opposed to their deficiencies), and that they enjoyed the challenge and learned more than on a traditional type of test.

Oral Interpersonal Performance Assessments

One type of performance assessment that is critical in assessing performance within the HLTPs presented in Volume I is the oral interpersonal assessment, in which the learner interacts with another learner or with the teacher to exchange ideas, address an issue, or solve a problem (see HLTP #2 in Volume I). Several studies across instructional levels have addressed student performance in assessments conducted across the three modes of communication. The university-level study conducted by Glisan et al. (2007) revealed that students did not perform as successfully on the interpersonal speaking tasks as they did on the presentational tasks (e.g., presenting a message or product to an audience of listeners or readers). As was found in the study completed at the secondary level by Adair-Hauck et al. (2006), spontaneous face-to-face interaction can be more daunting, given that it necessitates much classroom practice in which students must negotiate for meaning with others in a dynamic fashion. Nonetheless, in the Davin et al. study (2011) with fourth and fifth graders studying Spanish, performance was highest on the interpersonal mode, which the researchers attribute to the fact that the majority of class time for these students was devoted to oral communication. Nevertheless, across these studies, teachers acknowledged the need to include more spontaneous and open-ended types of situations that would allow students to interact with one another in meaningful ways. Further, they acknowledged the challenge involved in not only preparing students to engage in interpersonal tasks in the classroom but also in conducting these assessments while dealing with the realities of the classroom, such as large class size.

Modeling, Feedback, and Assessment Rubrics

While few would dispute the claim that feedback to learners is a critical factor in enabling progress to occur, learners report that they do not receive enough feedback that is helpful to their language development (Hyland & Hyland, 2006; Muñoz & Álvarez, 2010; Shohamy, Donitsa-Schmidt, & Ferman, 1996). In this regard, letter grades and vague comments such as 'good job' lack specific details regarding what learners are able to do at a given point in time and what they need to do to perform at the next level.

In the current paradigm for assessment as described above, **modeling** and **feedback** are pivotal in enabling students to improve and to assume greater responsibility for their own learning. As early as 1988, Tharpe and Gallimore described the critical nature of modeling as "a powerful means of assisting performance, one that continues its effectiveness into adult years and into the highest reaches of behavioral complexity" (1988, p. 49). In research on the Integrated Performance Assessment, for example, modeling was accomplished by showing learners recorded exemplars of students engaged in an oral interpersonal task; afterwards learners collaborated with the teacher to rate the performance using assessment rubrics (Adair-Hauck, Glisan, & Troyan, 2013; Adair-Hauck & Troyan, 2013).

A **rubric** has been defined by Wiggins and McTighe as "a criterion-based scoring guide consisting of a fixed measurement scale…and descriptions of the characteristics for each score point" (2005, p. 173). Rubrics feature a set of criteria and describe degrees of performance along a continuum ranging from 'exceeds expectations' to 'does not meet expectations.' To this end, rubrics present the criteria by which performance should be judged, illustrate the range of performance possible, and distinguish different levels of quality of performance. Hence rubrics are **criterion referenced**, inasmuch as learners are assessed against a set of criteria rather than being assessed in relation to other learners as in a norm-referenced system (i.e., 'on a bell curve'). Although rubrics have various types of formats, they all focus on measuring an outcome or performance, using a range to evaluate performance, and describing performance across the range in detail.

Sometimes the term 'rubric' is used erroneously to refer to any variation of a 'scoring guide,' such as the following one that might be used to assess speaking:

	Superior	**Good**	**Fair**	**Poor**
Content of message	4	3	2	1
Accuracy	4	3	2	1
Fluency	4	3	2	1
Comprehensibility	4	3	2	1
Use of communication strategies	4	3	2	1

However, the strict definition of the term 'rubric' refers to a tool that describes performance at each level across the range, as opposed to including numbers alone. In the example above, no description to match the numbers is provided, which not only makes it difficult to assign a rating but also to communicate clear and helpful expectations and feedback to learners.

Figure 4.1 depicts a rubric that uses the same criteria as those listed in the example above but provides the descriptions of performance across the levels. The descriptive and analytic nature of the rubric allows for assessment of individual criteria or performance

	Exceeds Expectations 4	**Meets Expectations-High 3**	**Meets Expectations-Low 2**	**Does Not Meet Expectations 1**
Completion of task; content of interaction	Exceeds task requirements and offers additional details; content of interaction pertinent	Completes task requirements; content of interaction pertinent	Completes the main parts of the task but lacks some details; content of interaction may not be fully pertinent	Does not complete main parts of the task and/ or content of interaction is not pertinent
Fluency	Speaks spontaneously with ease and natural pauses	Speaks spontaneously with a few pauses	Speaks spontaneously most of the time, but fluency breaks down occasionally	Speaks with pauses and hesitations that impede comprehensibility of interaction
Comprehensibility	Understood by those unaccustomed to dealing with L2 learners	Understood by those used to dealing with L2 learners; mostly understood by those unaccustomed to dealing with L2 learners	Understood by those used to dealing with L2 learners, but with some repetition and rephrasing	Understood with difficulty by those used to dealing with L2 learners
Accuracy (grammar & vocabulary)	85% or more of message accurate in terms of grammatical structures and vocabulary targeted	More than half of the message accurate in terms of grammatical structures and vocabulary targeted	At least half of the message accurate in terms of grammatical structures and vocabulary targeted	High degree of inaccuracy of grammar and/ or vocabulary impedes comprehensibility of interaction
Use of communicative strategies	Is an active participant in interaction; uses variety of strategies to negotiate meaning; responds fully to what partner says	Is an active participant in parts of interaction; uses expressions for negotiating meaning; makes several responses to what partner says	Is mostly reactive but uses expressions for negotiating meaning; makes at least one response to what partner says	Is reactive and makes few attempts to negotiate meaning; may not respond to what partner says

Figure 4.1. **Example of a Generic Analytic Rubric for Oral Interpersonal Speaking**

characteristics, which makes feedback clearer than is the case when using the type of scoring guide shown above. Another feature of this rubric is that it is **generic**, meaning that it can be used for multiple oral interpersonal tasks, given that it is not specific to one particular task. Finally, as is the case in many but not all rubrics, the rubric shown here includes an 'exceeds expectations' column in the range of performance. Because learners benefit from knowing what the next level of performance might be and what they would need to be able to do to reach that level, it is helpful to include this column on a rubric. To this end, it is always possible for some learners to exceed expectations in assessment tasks, in recognition of the fact that learners within a class typically demonstrate a wide range of performance abilities. However, novice teachers should note that, typically, few students perform at the 'exceeds expectations' level and that, for purposes of assigning grades, they would not need to do so for their performance to be considered in the 'A' range. See the next section for a fuller discussion of assigning grades and see the Deconstruction section for how to create a rubric.

Rubrics have become a useful tool in providing rich descriptions of performance across a range of performance levels (see more detailed discussion below and in Deconstruction section). More specifically, rubrics "show learners what good performance 'looks like' even before they perform an assessment task" (Shrum & Glisan, 2016, p. 380). Studies have shown that rubrics are not only helpful for teachers, but perhaps more importantly for learners, as they are better able to produce work of higher quality and feel less anxious about assignments and assessments than are their counterparts who do not receive rubrics (Andrade & Du, 2005).

As Stevens and Levi (2013) explain, rubrics enable teachers to provide timely feedback by using the performance descriptions as a springboard, and they serve as a tool for learners as they self-assess and engage in critical thinking to improve their performance. In this regard, rubrics are thought to 'level the playing field' by assisting *all* learners in understanding how they are performing and what they need to do to improve. Furthermore, teachers can use rubrics to collaborate with their colleagues and make decisions about common expectations in a course or program. Finally, because rubrics can be used to demonstrate learner progress over time and reveal strengths and weaknesses, they can also assist teachers in making changes to their teaching practices.

Along with modeling, exemplars, and rubrics, **descriptive feedback** is essential in improving learner performance. In fact, Hattie and Timperley (2007) identified feedback as one of the top five factors impacting achievement, with the most effective type of feedback being that of offering assistance to learners in the form of cues and reinforcement as well as providing connections to learning goals. Adair-Hauck and Troyan (2013) analyzed the use of **co-constructive feedback** on performance assessments, in which the teacher and learner engage in dialogue about learner performance. In such dialogic feedback sessions, the teacher and learner compare actual learner performance to model performance, as described in the rubrics and illustrated in the exemplars presented to learners before the assessment. This dialogic feedback is accomplished through assisting questions and cognitive probes posed by the teacher to coach the learner in reflecting upon and identifying strategies that would improve performance. The authors note that some learners may need assistance in brainstorming strategies for how they might improve their performance.

In sum, this research revealed that feedback that is socially constructed (i.e., negotiated in back-and-forth dialogue) between the teacher and the learner enables learners to become aware of and take responsibility for their own language development (see also Adair-Hauck, Glisan, & Troyan, 2013). This finding supports the types of dialogic contexts that are posited in the HLTPs presented in Volume I.

Although the use of the target language for instruction should be conducted 90% of the time in the target language, modeling and feedback are most often conducted in English (in classes where the majority of students speak English as their L1). One reason for this is that feedback should be fully comprehensible to learners and not create confusion through the use of complex language that they could not possibly know at their language level. Feedback requires learning about learning, a metacognitive process that is routinely carried out in the first language of even the most proficient bilingual and multilingual language users (e.g., numerical calculations, self-talk during complex tasks). A second reason is that, in the case of assessment, the use of English supports and facilitates the learning of the target language rather than preventing students from engaging with developmentally appropriate uses of the language during instruction (García, Johnson, & Seltzer, 2017).

Considerations about Conducting Contextualized Performance Assessments

(1) *Can't I just use the 'test' provided by the textbook program?* Before addressing this question, it would be helpful first to explore the difference between 'test' and 'assessment.' Although there is not a universal consensus on how to define these terms, the most popular definition of a **test** is a "method of measuring a person's ability, knowledge, or performance in a given domain" (Brown, 2004, p. 3). In this sense, a test is an instrument that focuses on specific abilities, knowledge, or performance in **domains** (i.e., sets of criteria) such as overall proficiency, knowledge of vocabulary, or pronunciation skill, and therefore represents assessment *of* learning, typically for summative purposes. In contrast, **assessment** is viewed as an ongoing process of collecting information regarding learner progress so that learning can be improved; thus, the goal is assessment *for* learning. The scope is much larger than that of a single test. In this regard, tests can be viewed as a subset of assessment but represent only one way in which a teacher can assess (Brown, 2004). Another way to view this distinction is that tests represent a 'retrospective' view by enabling teachers to look back at what students have achieved, while assessment is 'prospective' by enabling teachers to look forward by focusing on how instruction should unfold so that students can improve. As discussed earlier, although assessments can be implicit or explicit and can be used to make both formative and summative decisions, the *assessment process* that is intertwined with instruction will yield positive results in terms of student learning, motivation, and perceptions about learning.

While textbook programs might provide a series of 'tests,' they seldom address the larger realm of 'assessment' as defined above. Further, textbook 'tests' feature mostly discrete-point items that test knowledge of grammatical structures and vocabulary, are easily scoreable, and focus on paper-and-pencil formats as opposed to oral ones. They typically lack contextualization and meaningful use of language, and they rarely address the five goal areas of the national standards. Additionally, these prepared tests seldom fit the exact context that the teacher has designed for the unit, which presumably would include material that has been added beyond what is in the textbook (e.g., cultural perspectives, outcomes for oral interpersonal interaction, interpretive/discourse strategies). In sum, commercially-prepared tests that accompany textbooks should be examined carefully to determine whether they fit the instructional context and goals, and whether sections of them could be used in an adapted fashion. Either way, textbook tests are likely to address only part of the overall assessment approach that should be seamlessly connected to contextualized instruction.

(2) How do I know whether an oral assessment is interpersonal or not? As explained in HLTP #2 in Volume I, interpersonal speaking involves spontaneous interaction between at least two individuals, while presentational speaking is one-way communication, often scripted, between a speaker and an audience of listeners. Interpersonal speaking is motivated by a need to communicate within a meaningful context—e.g., information needs to be shared, a problem needs to be solved. In this regard, it involves negotiating a message in a back-and-forth manner so that meaning can be clarified and communication can move forward. Hence speakers use strategies for making themselves understood and for trying to understand what is being said by the other person. On the other hand, presentational speaking features talk that is 'one way' to an audience within a context where negotiation of meaning cannot typically occur (e.g., a prepared talk to an audience, a recorded scripted announcement). While effective presenters tailor their talk to the audience, seeking and offering clarification and confirmation in the moment do not usually occur in oral presentations.

Oral assessments that are interpersonal feature communicative tasks that are realized between two students or between the teacher and student, and they have the same characteristics as do oral interpersonal tasks conducted in class, as described above; see also HLTP #2 in Volume I. In short, one learner interacts with at least one other person for a real communicative purpose that drives the interaction, and they speak in a spontaneous manner—that is, *not* by reading a prepared script or reciting memorized material. As will be explained later, although the goal is for learners to interact spontaneously, they can be given some time to think and plan prior to the interaction and/or even to jot down a few notes. The point is that, for an oral assessment to be *interpersonal*, learners do *not* read from a prepared script. Given the nature of spontaneous communication, learners do not know in advance what the other person will say. In fact, this unknown characteristic of an interpersonal interaction is what prompts learners to use strategies to negotiate the meaning of what is said—e.g., asking for clarification of the message heard, providing additional details to explain one's own message.

(3) How can I administer an oral interpersonal assessment in a class of 30 learners? Conducting oral interpersonal assessments with large classes of learners undoubtedly poses challenges in terms of feasibility and requires several decisions for how to manage the classroom. While decisions about how these assessments are administered are context-dependent—i.e., they depend on the instructional context, students, and purposes of the assessments—there are several considerations that may assist teachers. First, realistically speaking, a typical oral assessment designed for pairs of students

might only take two minutes for each pair in a lower-level class and perhaps three to four minutes per pair in a higher-level one. Assessments can be administered over the course of multiple class days to accommodate a larger group. In the scenario described here, teachers with 30 learners would probably need a minimum of two class periods for class sessions that last approximately 40 minutes; teachers of block-scheduled classes (approximately 90 minutes) might be able to complete the assessment in one class period. While teachers may initially feel that 'this is a lot of time to devote to assessment,' it is important to remember that assessment *is* part of instruction, particularly when it is seamlessly connected to the learning process; therefore, it is worth the time dedicated to it. Secondly, logistical decisions must be made in terms of how to administer the assessment. In PK-12 settings, pairs of students can be taken to a corner of the classroom, or even right outside the classroom door if the school permits the teacher to supervise the rest of the class from the hallway. Some PK-12 teachers take students to a language or computer laboratory where they sit in cubicles and it is easier to monitor the class. Alternatively, pairs of students could interact simultaneously in a language or computer laboratory and record their interactions, or use other technologies such as Sound Cloud, which allows them to record on their phone and send the teacher the link to their recordings. Using technologies to record interactions, however, requires the teacher to spend a great deal of time listening to the recordings; in addition, students may become distracted with the surrounding noise of everyone speaking at once. In postsecondary settings, students can schedule appointments and go to the instructor's office for the oral assessments.

A third decision involves what to do with the rest of the class (in PK-12 settings) while pairs of students are engaged in the assessment, particularly since the teacher's attention must be focused on the performance. It is best to have students engaged in an activity that they view as being important as opposed to offering 'free time' that might lead to noise and even chaos. Some teachers have students wear earphones/headsets to watch a video that is related to the unit theme and/or will be used in some way in the future. If a project is underway, students can use the time to search the internet for information that they will ultimately use. If students periodically engage in independent work as part of class requirements, as in working on the self-assessment checklists that appear in the *NCSSFL-ACTFL Can-Do Statements* (ACTFL, 2013), they can be given time in class to make progress. Engaging learners in work that will 'count' and for which they will be given credit is a strategy to ensure on-task behavior while the assessment is under way.

(4) While it is easy to grade a discrete-point section of a test (e.g., grammar), how do I grade a performance assessment using a rubric? Rubrics take the mystery out of grading a performance and can save teachers a great deal of time in rating student performances and assigning grades. As will be explored in the Deconstruction section, creating a rubric from scratch takes time. However, as Stevens and Levi explain, "...the degree to which rubrics facilitate grading by avoiding repetition is in direct inverse ratio to how long it took us to create the rubric" (2013, p. 75). That is, although it often takes some time up front to design a rubric so that it includes the necessary feedback details for an assessment that has yet to take place, teachers save a great deal of time after the assessment has taken place, when they can rate performance using rich rubric descriptions

for each criterion listed—they merely need to mark the level of performance for each criterion. Further, rubric descriptions can serve as the basis for feedback dialogue sessions between the teacher and individual learners, as noted earlier, in addition to being used as the springboard for specific recommendations made to the learner regarding how to improve performance.

Although rubrics were originally intended as a tool for describing and rating performance, the reality of the educational world requires that performance on assessments be quantified in some way and that grades be assigned, regardless of the instructional level. There are many ways to assign points to rubric categories, to assign different weights to categories so as to make certain criteria worth more than others, to use a holistic system based on where ratings fall on the range of performance, and even to use a mathematical formula to derive a percentage or points that convert to a letter grade. A quick search on the internet will yield a number of ideas for how to derive grades from rubric scores; see also the text *Introduction to Rubrics* by Stevens & Levi (2013). Many school districts have their own systems for assigning grades from rubrics.

Whatever system is used, however, there is a huge caution for novice teachers, who may be tempted to calculate a grade by simply adding up points and dividing by the total number of points possible, as one might do on a paper-and-pencil test; e.g., a student receives 10 out of 20 points, which would be a 50% and most likely a failing grade. However, a typical rubric, especially one that includes an 'exceeds expectations' column, cannot be scored in this way. For example, in Figure 4.1 above, if a maximum of four points is assigned for each category, the total possible points would be 20. Using this rubric, a student could be rated in the Meets Expectations-Low column on all five criteria, which would be a total of 10 points. In the standard mathematical way of calculating a score, the student would receive 50% and fail the assessment. However, on the rubric, the student 'met expectations,' albeit at the low level, which could not be viewed as failing the assessment.

Although there are different ways to use rubrics to assign points and percentages, one popular method is the use of a mathematical equation. Because it is not possible for a student to score a zero on the type of rubric shown in Figure 4.1, the teacher must decide what the minimum passing score would be (e.g., 60%). An equation then converts the rubric points to a range of percentages between the highest possible (100%) and lowest possible (e.g., 60%). As explained by Shrum and Glisan (2016, p. 386), the following equation would be used for the rubric in Figure 4.1, which has a maximum of 20 points possible:

$$(\text{Total points x } 52)/20 + 48 = \_\_\_\_\_\%.$$

In the example given above of a student earning 10 points (all in the 'meets expectations-low' category) on a 20-point rubric, the grade would be 74%, which would most likely represent a letter grade of C or C-. Teachers might also use a Web site called Roobrix (http://www.roobrix.com), which computes the score based on the data entered regarding the number of criteria and the lowest passing grade.

(5) *Can I just use an existing rubric that I find online? Can a rubric ever be changed?* It is easy to find a wealth of ready-made rubrics in publications and online, and often they can serve as examples that may assist teachers in creating their own. However, as Stevens and Levi warn, seldom can any ready-made rubric be used as is, since it was not designed specifically to fit either the assessment task or the expectations of the learners for whom it will be used. They suggest that the decision to use an existing rubric depends on two related issues: time and suitability. First, is there time to adapt the rubric to fit the task and performance expectations? Second, how suitable is the rubric for the specific performance task a teacher has designed for students? (2013, p. 106). Teachers will undoubtedly find it necessary to examine a ready-made rubric carefully by reflecting on the degree to which it addresses the learning objectives and expectations of the performance task and what language on the rubric could be used and/or modified for use with a particular task and the students. In sum, although existing rubrics can offer ideas and language that might be helpful in creating a rubric or serve as a springboard for a teacher's own rubric, it is unlikely that they can be adopted for use without taking substantial time to modify them.

A rubric created from scratch is also in a constant state of being revised. In this regard, the process of developing a rubric depends on the analysis of student performance against the characteristics of performance depicted on each level of the rubric. As samples of student performance are collected, the teacher applies the rubric descriptors to assign ratings. This process will reveal that some parts of the rubric may work well but other parts may need to be tweaked for future use. Teachers add and/or change descriptions so that they contain more precise language and can be used more effectively to assess student performance. As explained by Wiggins and McTighe, "...a rubric is never complete until it has been used to evaluate student work *and* an analysis of different levels of work is used to sharpen the descriptors" (2005, p. 180). Another reason for close analysis of student work in relation to the rubric is to find **anchors**—that is, examples of student performance that serve as concrete examples of performance on each level of a rubric. These anchors can then be shown to learners on the next iteration of an assessment to illustrate models of performance and serve as a link to classroom instruction. In this way, the rubric becomes a pivotal link in the seamless connection between instruction and assessment. In short, rubrics are dynamic in nature and are always evolving to reflect the realities of student performance and to accurately describe expectations for performance.

In the following sections, the three small-grain-size practices are deconstructed. As a reminder, the assessments presented here are formats that would be part of a larger repertoire of assessment practices, and they were selected in part because of their relationship to the other HLTPs.

Deconstructing the Practice: Creating and Administering Oral Interpersonal Performance Assessments

Deconstructing this practice involves considering it from two perspectives: (1) creating an oral interpersonal performance assessment, and (2) administering the oral interpersonal assessment. *Creating an oral interpersonal performance assessment* is accomplished through the following steps, which can be applied using the Oral Interpersonal Performance Assessment Planning Template in Figure 4.2. This template is very similar to the Oral Interpersonal Task Planning Template found in Figure 2.2, HLTP #2 (see Volume I), and this similarity exemplifies the seamless connection between instruction and assessment.

- Identify the specific objective(s) from the unit of instruction as well as the language functions that this assessment will address (see HLTP #8).
- Identify the goal areas and standards from the *World-Readiness Standards for Learning Languages* (National Standards Collaborative Board, 2015) to be addressed in the assessment.
- Identify the meaningful context in which the assessment will take place (see HLTP #7).
- Design a task that pairs of students will complete by talking to each other using the target language. Be sure that the task reflects the type of instructional experiences learners have had within this context.
- Identify the key grammatical structures and vocabulary that may naturally occur in the assessment task.
- Decide how this task will contribute to the larger inquiry question of the unit.
- Identify the communication strategies learners will need to use as they engage in the assessment (e.g., negotiating for meaning, offering or asking for clarification, requesting additional information).
- Prepare the task by printing instructions for Student A on one card or paper and instructions for Student B on a separate card or paper. Instructions should be written in English so that learners understand the task and so that key target language vocabulary is not revealed to them on the card.
- Create a rubric for the assessment. This is a separate small-grain practice that will be deconstructed in a later section in this chapter, including how to make decisions regarding providing feedback to learners after the performance is assessed.
- Prepare learners for the assessment by suggesting that they review vocabulary, communicative strategies, and grammar specific to the objectives and functions to be addressed in the assessment. Although learners should not be given the exact assessment task, they should be given guidance regarding how they might prepare for the interaction.

Oral Interpersonal Assessment Planning Template

Language & Level of Class:

Objectives/Functions addressed in assessment:

Goal areas and standards from the *World-Readiness Standards for Learning Languages* addressed in assessment:

Meaningful context for assessment:

Assessment Task:

Student A:

Student B:

Key vocabulary for the assessment:

Key grammatical structures for the assessment:

How task contributes to larger inquiry question:

Targeted communication strategies:

How performance will be assessed (i.e., rubric categories):

How learners will be prepared for the assessment:

***Figure 4.2.* Oral Interpersonal Performance Assessment Planning Template**

In HLTP #8, an example was given of a context based on the inquiry question, 'How do cultural norms influence our concept of good nutrition?' One functional objective based on this question is 'To compare cross-cultural beliefs about what constitutes healthy eating habits.' Figure 4.3 illustrates an example of an oral interpersonal assessment task that could address this objective as well as the inquiry question. See Figure 4.1 for an example of a rubric that could be used to assess this task, and further discussion of rubrics later in this chapter.

The Nutrition Dilemma — Student A

You are thinking about trying out the Mediterranean diet to improve your eating habits. You strike up a conversation with a friend to see what they know about this diet and what they think about it. Initiate the conversation and inquire about what your friend knows about the diet and whether they think it would be good to try it. Share what you know about it also and share information about the nutrition habits that both of you have. You have two minutes to share as much as you can about this situation. Be sure to react to what your friend says and ask for more details when necessary.

The Nutrition Dilemma — Student B

Your friend wants to talk to you about a new diet they hope to try. Respond with what you know about the diet and what your opinions are about it. Share information about the nutrition habits that both of you have. You have two minutes to share as much as you can about this situation. Be sure to react to what your friend says and ask for more details when necessary.

***Figure 4.3.* Example of an Oral Interpersonal Assessment Task**

Administering the oral interpersonal assessment is based on the following considerations:

1. Decide how many minutes to allow for the task—many instructors, for example, give a maximum of two minutes to complete the interaction.
2. Decide when the assessment will be given. Can it be completed during one class session or over the course of multiple class days? In the case of postsecondary settings, when will learners visit the instructor's office (i.e., sign up for appointments)?
3. Decide what the rest of the class will do while pairs of students are completing the assessment. See suggestions under Question #3 in the previous section.
4. Decide how students will be placed in pairs—i.e., will students be paired randomly, or will the teacher assign specific students to work together? The fairest strategy may be to pair them randomly given that, in the world beyond the classroom, they will be faced with interacting with many different types of speakers, including those who may speak at higher or lower levels of proficiency.
5. Decide where pairs of students will go to complete the assessment. A corner of the classroom? Right outside of the classroom door? The instructor's office?
6. Give each pair one or two minutes to read their cards/papers and have some time to think about the task before beginning the assessment.
7. Have rubrics ready so that you can take notes and assess each performance while observing the interaction. As an option, record some assessments so that there is a record of performance and so that learners can hear their performance during a feedback session with the teacher.

Deconstructing the Practice: Creating Presentational Writing Assessments

Although presentational writing assessments can have various formats, we are presenting a genre-based writing assessment to support functional meaning making and to further illustrate how instruction and assessment should be seamlessly connected. As was explained in Chapter 3 on HLTP #9, genre enables learners to write purposefully to achieve a goal in social and cultural contexts (Schleppegrell, Moore, Al-Adeimi, O'Hallron, Palincsar, & Symons, 2014). Creating a genre-based presentational writing assessment is accomplished through the following steps, which can be applied using the Planning Template for Creating a Genre-based Presentational Writing Assessment in Figure 4.4. The similarity between this template and the planning part of the Tool for Planning and Teaching a Genre-Based Presentational Writing Lesson found in Figure 3.3 in the previous chapter illustrates the connection between instruction and assessment.

1. Identify the specific objective(s) from the unit of instruction as well as language functions that this assessment will address (see HLTPs #8 and #9).
2. Identify the goal areas and standards from the *World-Readiness Standards for Learning Languages* (National Standards Collaborative Board, 2015) to be addressed in the assessment.
3. Identify the meaningful context in which the assessment will take place (see HLTPs #7 and #9).
4. Select the genre that will be the focus of the writing assessment and the targeted audience for the written product.
5. Identify the stages of the genre to be assessed.
6. Design the genre-based task.
7. Identify the key grammatical structures and vocabulary to be targeted in the assessment.
8. Decide how this task will contribute to the larger inquiry question of the unit.
9. Create instructions for the task: Stipulate the genre, audience, meaningful goal, scope/length of the product, and grammatical structures/vocabulary that should be included.
10. Create a rubric for the assessment. This is a separate small-grain practice that will be deconstructed in a later section in this chapter, including how to make decisions regarding providing feedback to learners after the performance is assessed.
11. Prepare learners for the assessment by suggesting that they review the genre(s) studied in the unit and the vocabulary and grammar specific to the objectives and functions to be addressed.

Planning Template for Creating a
Genre-Based Presentational Writing Assessment

Language & Level of Class:

Objectives/Functions addressed in assessment:

Goal areas and standards from the *World-Readiness Standards for Learning Languages* addressed in assessment:

Meaningful context for assessment:

Genre:

Targeted Audience:

Stages of the Genre to be Assessed:

Assessment Task:

Key vocabulary for the assessment:

Key grammatical structures for the assessment:

How task contributes to larger inquiry question:

How performance will be assessed (i.e., rubric categories):

How learners will be prepared for the assessment:

***Figure 4.4.* Planning Template for Creating a Genre-based Presentational Writing Assessment**

Figure 4.5 depicts a sample genre-based presentational writing assessment task that could be given as a part of the unit on nutrition.

Genre-Based Presentational Writing Assessment Task

Genre: Giving instructions for living a healthy lifestyle
Audience: Readers of student newspaper

Imagine that you are a writer for the Spanish section ("Food and Daily Living") of your student newspaper. Create an article of 3 paragraphs (approximately 250 words) in which you provide instructions for how to live a healthy lifestyle. Remember that instructions often include steps to achieve a goal and each step tells us what we need to do and do next. The text may also include comments on the reason, importance, or usefulness of each step. Use the format for giving instructions that you learned in the unit, as well as vocabulary for foods, diets, and daily activities. Incorporate action verbs in the present indicative and the subjunctive to offer suggestions and make recommendations. Detailed information on health lifestyle practices should also be provided, for example, how (with a positive attitude), where (outdoor and indoor exercise) and when (at least 3 days a week). Be sure to add a title that entices readers to read your article!

***Figure 4.5.* Example of a Genre-Based Presentational Writing Assessment Task**

Deconstructing the Practice: Providing Feedback to Learners Through Performance Assessment Rubrics

Deconstructing this practice entails two phases: (1) creating the performance assessment rubric, and (2) using the performance assessment rubric to provide feedback to learners. *Creating the performance assessment rubric* can be accomplished by means of the steps described below, which represent one approach. Teachers may find other strategies for designing rubrics in published literature and pedagogical materials. As indicated earlier, the most effective type of rubric is one that is designed specifically to meet particular tasks and learner expectations, as opposed to a ready-made one that is found online and used without any modifications.

1. Examine the performance task and determine the learner-centered objectives that drive it. For example, in an oral interpersonal task such as the one in Figure 4.3, learners might ask questions, use strategies for maintaining the conversation, discuss and/or discover specific information in the oral exchange, and use particular grammatical structures that support meaning-making.
2. Create a set of three to five of the most important performance criteria that relate to these objectives. Criteria are usually listed in the form of nouns and may be either generic or task-specific. Generic criteria are often used for a specific mode of communication such as oral interpersonal speaking or presentational writing and may be used for multiple performance tasks; examples of these criteria are 'use of conversational strategies,' 'completion of task requirements,' 'accuracy/quality of language use', and 'fluency.' See Figure 4.1 for sample criteria in a generic rubric. Examples of task-specific criteria for the performance task shown in Figure 4.3 could include 'knowledge of the Mediterranean diet,' 'question asking,' and 'use of expressive reactions.'
3. Decide how many levels of performance the rubric will have. While there is no set number of levels a rubric should include, most have between three and five. Stevens and Levi (2013) suggest the use of three levels when first constructing a rubric and then expanding it to four or five levels after it has been used for an actual assignment. Including more than five levels makes it difficult to differentiate between them and to identify why a student's work is rated at a particular level. Shrum and Glisan (2016) suggest four levels to avoid having most students' performances fall into the middle level.
4. Decide how the performance levels will be labeled. Examples of labels include "Exceeds Expectations, Meets Expectations-Strong, Meets Expectations-Weak, Does Not Meet Expectations" (Adair-Hauck, Glisan, & Troyan, 2013, p. 126), or "Exemplary, Accomplished, Developing, Beginning" (Stevens & Levi, 2013, p. 200). Arrange the levels by listing the highest level on the far left-hand side of the rubric and proceeding down the range until the lowest level is on the far right-hand side.
5. Write the performance descriptions for each level. The descriptions should contain the most important defining characteristics and be written in student-friendly language. Begin with the highest level by asking, 'What type of performance would exceed the expectations that the teacher has for the majority of students?' As explained

earlier, one of the benefits of a rubric is that it shows the next level of performance toward which students can work. After defining the highest level, describe what the lowest (i.e., unacceptable) performance would be, and then create the levels in between. This process typically involves going back and forth between levels to tweak the language of the descriptions. To the extent possible, try to avoid comparative language such as *fewer, more/less than*, as well as numbers (of expressions, sentences, or other features) and adverbs such as *frequently, mostly, seldom*, which place emphasis on quantity instead of quality of work.

6. Provide room on the rubric sheet for written feedback by the teacher. Helpful feedback gives a rationale for why performance was rated a certain way and offers suggestions for improvement. As mentioned earlier, this feedback can be used in face-to-face dialogic feedback sessions with individual learners.
7. After the rubric is used to assess a performance task, revise it accordingly to define performance more accurately. Rubrics are in a constant state of modification as student exemplars are used to tweak criteria and performance descriptions on them.

Using the performance assessment rubric to provide feedback to learners is the second part of the deconstruction of this practice.

1. Prior to administering the assessment task, show the rubric to learners so that they understand performance expectations. Discuss the task criteria and levels of performance with learners and answer any questions they might have.
2. Along with the rubric, present samples or exemplars of student work that was done in the past—also called 'anchors'—to help learners to see what performance is like at each level of the performance continuum on the rubric (Wiggins & McTighe, 2005). To enable this phase of the process to occur, teachers should try to keep copies of student work (with names and any other identifying information removed) that can be shown to future students. Sharing and discussing these anchors is a critical part of the process of assisting learners in understanding expectations.
3. After the assessment, identify the level of performance for each criterion on the rubric and provide written feedback (see #6 above). Assign a grade for each learner's performance (see the discussion about assigning grades to rubrics in the Considerations section above). Return scored rubrics as soon as possible and have a class discussion about learners' performance in general, providing time for questions. It is advisable to provide time for individual dialogic feedback sessions for at least some of the performance tasks so that learners can gain more from discussion with the teacher on their own progress.

In sum, the two types of assessments presented here, together with rubric design, are formats that would be part of a larger repertoire of assessment practices. A robust assessment plan addresses multiple learning outcomes and goal areas of the standards, as well as including a variety of assessment types. Finally, although only the interpersonal and presentational modes have been presented in this chapter, the interpretive mode should also be assessed within the larger assessment plan.

Rehearsing the Practice

The following tasks are provided to practice ways to develop contextualized performance-based assessments.

1. Select a textbook test or a test provided by your instructor. Evaluate the effectiveness of the test by considering the following questions and providing details to explain your responses:
   - Does the test have a meaningful context?
   - Is the test performance-based?
   - What learning outcomes does the test assess?
   - Is any part of the test oral in nature? If so, are learners asked to interact in a communicative fashion with another person?
   - If necessary, how could you adapt this test to make it more meaningful and performance-based?
2. Review the oral interpersonal assessment depicted in Figure 4.3 above. Complete the planning template in Figure 4.2 to show how it could have been used to plan this assessment.
3. Use the planning template in Figure 4.2 to design an oral interpersonal assessment. If you are currently teaching or participating in a field experience in a K-12 classroom, you might design an assessment that you can administer to your learners. Another option is to design an oral assessment that would fit into the context you selected in Chapter 2, Rehearsing the Practice, #2. You might find it helpful to refer to External Mediational Tools #10A and #10B as you design and administer this assessment.
4. Use the planning template in Figure 4.4 to design a genre-based presentational writing assessment task. If you are currently teaching or participating in a field experience in a K-12 classroom, you might design an assessment that you can administer to your learners. Another option is to design an assessment that would fit into the context you selected in Chapter 2, Rehearsing the Practice, #2. You might find it helpful to refer to External Mediational Tool #10C as you design this assessment.
5. Design a performance assessment rubric for one of the assessments you developed in #3 and #4 above. Refer to External Mediational Tool #10D as you create the rubric. If you are currently teaching or participating in a field experience in a K-12 classroom, you might design a rubric that you can use with an assessment for your learners; refer to External Mediational Tool #10E as you use the rubric with your learners.

Assessing the Practice

Use Rubric #10 in Appendix 4-B to self-assess the assessments and rubrics that you developed in #3, #4, and #5 above. As an alternative or in addition, you could ask a colleague to review an assessment that you have created and provide feedback using the appropriate categories on the rubric.

Putting the Practice into a Larger Context: Instructional Goals and Challenges

Assessing learner performance is a high-leverage practice that permeates all subject areas. Teaching Works, which grew out of the Teacher Education Initiative (TEI) at the University of Michigan, identified a total of 19 HLTPs, four of which deal with assessment of learner performance:

- #15 Checking student understanding during and at the conclusion of lessons
- #16 Selecting and designing formal assessments of student learning
- #17 Interpreting the results of student work, including routine assignments, quizzes, tests, projects, and standardized assessments
- #18 Providing oral and written feedback to students (Teaching Works, 2020).

Beyond these generic practices, virtually all subject areas have also identified assessing student performance as a high-leverage practice; see, for example, history education (Kennedy, 2016); mathematics education (Sleep, 2009); and special education (Council for Exceptional Children and CEEDAR Center, 2017).

Developing contextualized performance assessments supports current views in the larger educational field regarding the need to integrate instruction and assessment in a seamless fashion (Adair-Hauck, Glisan, & Troyan, 2013; Wiggins, 1998; Wiggins & McTighe, 2005); the important role of modeling and feedback within a learning community (Hattie & Timperley, 2007); and the role of the teacher as a collaborative mediator with the learner instead of a solitary evaluator of performance (Poehner, 2007). In this regard, assessment of student learning that is woven seamlessly into instruction undergirds all other teaching practices. Decisions about assessment are made early in the instructional planning process (see HLTP #8) and assessment is couched within a meaningful and purposeful context (see HLTP #7). In Volume I, the role of assessment within the first six HLTPs was mentioned. A critical aspect of assessment as explored in this chapter is the feedback negotiated by the teacher with learners within a dialogic context, with the use of modeling, student exemplars for discussion, and rubrics. It bears repeating that providing dialogic feedback within a sociocultural approach is pivotal to mediating language learning, development, and performance. Hence, the practice of assessing learner performance in this way is central to learners' linguistic, cognitive, and social development and contributes to the building of a discourse community in which the teacher and learners work together to improve performance.

In addition to reflecting contemporary views regarding the close connection between instruction and assessment, this HLTP addresses larger teaching challenges. First, in a more traditional approach to assessment, learners do not always see the connection between their classroom experiences and assessments. Linking assessment to instruction enables learners to recognize the connection between their classroom experiences and what they are asked to do on performance assessments, which has been found to have a positive effect on learners' motivation for and perceptions about language learning (Glisan, Uribe, & Adair-Hauck, 2007; Zapata, 2016). Secondly, dialogic feedback encourages learners to self-assess and to think actively about what they are learning and about the role they have in their own learning and development (Kennedy, 2016). Thirdly, through this approach learners become members of a learning community in which they collaborate with the teacher, who is viewed as a joint problem solver and coach. Finally, this view of assessment serves as an impetus for teachers to transform and improve their classroom practices so that learners' performance can improve.

References

Adair-Hauck, B., Glisan, E. W., Koda, K., Swender, E. B., & Sandrock, P. (2006). The Integrated Performance Assessment (IPA): Connecting assessment to instruction and learning. *Foreign Language Annals, 39,* 359-382.

Adair-Hauck, B., Glisan, E. W., & Troyan, F. J. (2013). *Implementing Integrated Performance Assessment.* Alexandria, VA: ACTFL.

Adair-Hauck, B., & Troyan, F. J. (2013). A descriptive and co-constructive approach to Integrated Performance Assessment feedback. *Foreign Language Annals, 46,* 23-44.

American Council on the Teaching of Foreign Languages (ACTFL). (2012). *ACTFL proficiency guidelines.* Alexandria, VA: Author. Retrieved from http://www.actfl.org/publications/guidelines-and-manuals/actfl-proficiency-guidelines-2012

American Council on the Teaching of Foreign Languages (ACTFL). (2013). *NCSSFL-ACTFL can-do statements.* Alexandria, VA: Author. Retrieved from http://www.actfl.org/publications/guidelines-and-manuals/ncssfl-actfl-can-do-statements

Andrade, H., & Du, Y. (2005). Student perspectives on rubric-referenced assessment. *Practical Assessment, Research & Evaluation, 10,* 1-11.

Bachman, L. F. (2007). What is the construct? The dialectic of abilities and contexts in defining constructs in language assessment. In J. Fox, M. Wesche, & D. Bayliss (Eds.), *What are we measuring? Language testing reconsidered* (pp. 41-71). Ottawa: University of Ottawa Press.

Bachman, L. F., & Palmer, A. (2010). *Language assessment in practice.* Oxford: Oxford University Press.

Brown, H. D. (2004). *Language assessment: Principles and classroom practice.* White Plains, NY: Pearson.

Council for Exceptional Children & Collaboration for Effective Educator Development, Accountability and Reform (CEEDAR) Center. (2017). *High-leverage practices in special education.* Retrieved from https://ceedar.education.ufl.edu/wp-content/uploads/2017/07/CEC-HLP-Web.pdf

Davin, K. J., Troyan, F. J., Donato, R., & Hellmann, A. (2011). Research on the Integrated Performance Assessment in an early foreign language learning program. *Foreign Language Annals, 44,* 605-625.

García, O., Johnson, S. I., & Seltzer, K. (2017). *The translanguaging classroom: Leveraging student bilingualism for learning.* Philadelphia: Caslon.

Glisan, E. W., Uribe, D., & Adair-Hauck, B. (2007). Research on Integrated Performance Assessment at the post-secondary level: Student performance across the modes of communication. *Canadian Modern Language Review, 64,* 39-68.

Hattie, J., & Timperley, H. (2007). The power of feedback. *Review of Educational Research, 77,* 81-112.

Hyland, K., & Hyland, F. (2006). Feedback on second language students' writing. *Language Teaching,* 39, 83-101.

Kennedy, M. (2016). Parsing the practice of teaching. *Journal of Teacher Education, 67*(1), 6-17.

Kissau, S., & Adams, M. J. (2016). Instructional decision making and IPAs: Assessing the modes of communication. *Foreign Language Annals, 49,* 105-123.

Liskin-Gasparro, J. E. (1996). Assessment: From content standards to student performance. In R. C. Lafayette (Ed.), National standards: A catalyst for reform. *The ACTFL Foreign Language Education Series* (pp. 169-196). Lincolnwood, IL: NTC/Contemporary.

McNamara, T. (2001). Language assessment as social practice: Challenges for research. *Language Testing, 18,* 334-339.

Muñoz, A. P., & Álvarez, M. E. (2010). Washback of an oral assessment system in the EFL classroom. *Language Testing, 27,* 33-49.

National Standards in Foreign Language Education Project (NSFLEP). (1996). *Standards for foreign language learning: Preparing for the 21st century.* Lawrence, KS: Allen Press.

National Standards in Foreign Language Education Project (NSFLEP). (1999). *Standards for foreign language learning in the 21st century (SFLL).* Lawrence, KS: Allen Press.

National Standards in Foreign Language Education Project (NSFLEP). (2006). *Standards for foreign language learning in the 21st century (SFLL).* Lawrence, KS: Allen Press.

National Standards Collaborative Board. (2015). *World-readiness standards for learning languages* (4th ed.). Alexandria, VA: Author.

Poehner, M. E. (2007). Beyond the test: L2 dynamic assessment and the transcendence of mediated learning. *Modern Language Journal,* 91, 323–340.

Poehner, M. E., & Lantolf, J. P. (2003). *Dynamic assessment of L2 development: Bringing the past into the future.* CALPER Working Papers Series, No. I. The Pennsylvania State University, Center for Advanced Language Proficiency, Education and Research.

Purpura, J. E. (2016). Second and foreign language assessment. *Foreign Language Annals, 100,* 190-208.

Schleppegrell, M. J., Moore, J., Al-Adeimi, S., O'Hallaron, C. L., Palincsar, A. S., & Symons, C. (2014). Tackling a genre: Situating SFL genre pedagogy in a new context. In L. C. de Oliveira & J. Iddings (Eds.), *Genre pedagogy across curriculum* (pp. 26-39). Bristol, CT: Equinox.

Shohamy, E. (2001). *The power of tests: A critical perspective on the uses of language tests.* London: Pearson.

Shohamy, E. (2006). *Language policy: Hidden agendas and new approaches.* London: Routledge.

Shohamy, E., Donitsa-Schmidt, S., & Ferman, I. (1996). Test impact revisited: Washback effect over time. *Language Testing, 13*, 298-317.

Shrum, J. L., & Glisan, E. W. (2016). *Teacher's handbook: Contextualized language instruction* (5th ed.). Boston: Cengage Learning.

Sleep, L. (2009). *Teaching to the mathematical point: Knowing and using mathematics in teaching.* Unpublished doctoral dissertation. University of Michigan, Ann Arbor.

Stevens, D. D., & Levi, A. J. (2013). *Introduction to rubrics.* Sterling, VA: Stylus.

Struyven, K., Dochy, F., & Janssens, S. (2005). Students' perceptions about evaluation and assessment in higher education: A review. *Assessment and Evaluation in Higher Education, 30,* 331-347.

TeachingWorks. (2020). *High-leverage practices.* Retrieved from http://www.teachingworks.org/work-of-teaching/high-leverage-practices

Tharpe, R. G., & Gallimore, R. (1988). *Rousing minds to life: Teaching, learning, and schooling in social contexts.* New York: Cambridge University Press.

Troyan, F. J. (2012). Research on the National Standards: Defining the constructs and researching learner outcomes. *Foreign Language Annals, 45,* s118–s140. doi: 10.1111/j.1944-9720.2012.01182.x

Wiggins, G. (1993). *Assessing student performance.* San Francisco: Jossey-Bass.

Wiggins, G. (1998). *Educative assessment.* San Francisco: Jossey-Bass.

Wiggins, G., & McTighe, J. (2005). *Understanding by design.* Alexandria, VA: Association for Supervision and Curriculum Development.

Zapata, G. C. (2016). University students' perceptions of Integrated Performance Assessment and the connection between classroom learning and assessment. *Foreign Language Annals, 49,* 93-104.

Appendix 4-A-a

External Mediational Tool #10A: Creating an Oral Interpersonal Performance Assessment

1. Identify the specific objective(s) from the unit of instruction as well as the language functions that this assessment will address (see HLTP #8).
2. Identify the goal areas and standards from the *World-Readiness Standards for Learning Languages* to be addressed in the assessment.
3. Identify the meaningful context in which the assessment will take place (see HLTP #7).
4. Design a task that pairs of students will complete by talking to each other using the target language. Be sure that the task reflects the type of instructional experiences learners have had within this context.
5. Identify the key grammatical structures and vocabulary that may naturally occur in the assessment task.
6. Decide how this task will contribute to the larger inquiry question of the unit.
7. Identify the communication strategies learners will need to use as they engage in the assessment (e.g., negotiating for meaning, offering or asking for clarification, requesting additional information).
8. Prepare the task by printing instructions for Student A on one card or paper and instructions for Student B on a separate card or paper. Instructions should be written in English so that learners understand the task and so that key target language vocabulary is not revealed to them on the card.
9. Create a rubric for the assessment.
10. Prepare learners for the assessment by suggesting that they review vocabulary, communicative strategies, and grammar specific to the objectives and functions to be addressed in the assessment. Although learners should not be given the exact assessment task, they should be given guidance regarding how they might prepare for the interaction.

Appendix 4-A-b

External Mediational Tool #10B: Administering an Oral Interpersonal Performance Assessment

1. Decide how many minutes to allow for the task.
2. Decide when the assessment will be given. Can it be completed during one class session or over the course of multiple class days? In the case of postsecondary settings, when will learners visit the instructor's office (i.e., sign up for appointments)?
3. Decide what the rest of the class will do while pairs of students are completing the assessment.
4. Decide how students will be placed in pairs—i.e., will students be paired randomly or will the teacher assign specific students to work together?
5. Decide where pairs of students will go to complete the assessment. A corner of the classroom? Right outside of the classroom door? The instructor's office?
6. Give each pair one or two minutes to read their cards/papers and have some time to think about the task before beginning the assessment.
7. Have rubrics ready so that you can take notes and assess each performance while observing the interaction.

Appendix 4-A-c

External Mediational Tool #10C: Creating a Genre-Based Presentational Writing Assessment

1. Identify the specific objective(s) from the unit of instruction as well as language functions that this assessment will address (see HLTPs #8 and #9).
2. Identify the goal areas and standards from the *World-Readiness Standards for Learning Languages* to be addressed in the assessment.
3. Identify the meaningful context in which the assessment will take place (see HLTPs #7 and #9).
4. Select the genre that will be the focus of the writing assessment and the targeted audience for the written product.
5. Identify the stages of the genre to be assessed.
6. Design the genre-based task.
7. Identify the key grammatical structures and vocabulary to be targeted in the assessment.
8. Decide how this task will contribute to the larger inquiry question of the unit.
9. Create instructions for the task: Stipulate the genre, audience, meaningful goal, scope/length of the product, and grammatical structures/vocabulary that should be included.
10. Create a rubric for the assessment.
11. Prepare learners for the assessment by suggesting that they review the genre(s) studied in the unit and the vocabulary and grammar specific to the objectives and functions to be addressed.

Appendix 4-A-d

External Mediational Tool #10D:
Creating a Performance Assessment Rubric

1. Examine the performance task and determine the learner-centered objectives that drive it.
2. Create a set of three to five of the most important performance criteria that relate to these objectives.
3. Decide how many levels of performance the rubric will have. While there is no set number of levels a rubric should include, most have between three and five.
4. Decide how the performance levels will be labeled. Arrange the levels by listing the highest level on the far left-hand side of the rubric and proceeding down the range until the lowest level is on the far right-hand side.
5. Write the performance descriptions for each level. The descriptions should contain the most important defining characteristics and be written in student-friendly language. Begin with the highest level by asking, 'What type of performance would exceed the expectations that the teacher has for the majority of students?' After defining the highest level, describe what the lowest (i.e., unacceptable) performance would be, and then create the levels in between. This process typically involves going back and forth between levels to tweak the language of the descriptions. To the extent possible, try to avoid comparative language such as *fewer, more/ less than,* as well as numbers (of expressions, sentences, or other features) and adverbs such as *frequently, mostly, seldom,* which place emphasis on quantity instead of quality of work.
6. Provide room on the rubric sheet for written feedback by the teacher. Helpful feedback gives a rationale for why performance was rated a certain way and offers suggestions for improvement. This feedback can be used in face-to-face dialogic feedback sessions with individual learners.
7. After the rubric is used to assess a performance task, revise it accordingly to define performance more accurately.

Appendix 4-A-e

External Mediational Tool #10E:
Using the Performance Assessment Rubric to Provide Feedback to Learners

1. Prior to administering the assessment task, show the rubric to learners so that they understand performance expectations. Discuss the task criteria and levels of performance with learners and answer any questions they might have.
2. Along with the rubric, present samples or exemplars of student work that was done in the past—also called 'anchors'—to help learners to see what performance is like at each level of the performance continuum on the rubric. Sharing and discussing these anchors is a critical part of the process of assisting learners in understanding expectations.
3. After the assessment, identify the level of performance for each criterion on the rubric and provide written feedback. Assign a grade for each learner's performance. Return scored rubrics as soon as possible and have a class discussion about learners' performance in general, providing time for questions. It is advisable to provide time for individual dialogic feedback sessions for at least some of the performance tasks so that learners can gain more from discussion with the teacher on their own progress.

Appendix 4-B

RUBRIC FOR HLTP #10: Developing Contextualized Performance Assessments

	Exceeds Expectations	Meets Expectations	Developing	Unacceptable
Integration of Assessment and Instruction	Assessment and instruction are closely intertwined. Assessments are planned and created before instructional experiences are planned. Both formative and summative assessments occur throughout instruction and focus on learner performance.	Assessment and instruction are intertwined. Assessments are planned, but not necessarily created, before instructional experiences are planned. Both formative and summative assessments occur throughout instruction and include tasks that elicit learner performance.	Assessment is connected to instruction. Assessments may be planned and created after instruction is complete. Both formative and summative assessments occur and include tasks that elicit learner performance.	Assessment is superficially connected to instruction. Assessments are planned and created after instruction is complete. Assessments are primarily summative and may or may not include tasks that elicit learner performance.
Contextualization of Assessments	Assessments occur within meaningful contexts, reflect learner outcomes, and elicit communicative target language performances.	Assessments include meaningful tasks, reflect learner outcomes, and elicit some communicative target language performances.	Assessments include meaningful tasks but do not consistently reflect learner outcomes. There is limited elicitation of communicative target language performances.	Assessments lack meaningful contexts and focus on discrete linguistic points. Elicitation of communicative target language performances is minimal or absent.
Goal areas/ Standards Addressed in Assessments	Assessments feature the goal areas and standards addressed in instruction. Assessment of oral interpersonal communication plays a prominent role.	Assessments feature most of the goal areas and standards addressed in instruction. Assessment of oral interpersonal communication is included.	Assessments tend to focus mostly on the Communication goal area. Limited assessment of oral interpersonal communication is included, and/or oral communication is presentational.	Assessments focus on grammar and vocabulary rather than on goal areas and standards. Oral interpersonal assessment is lacking.
Role of Feedback on Assessments	Feedback is central to instruction and assessment. Teacher uses modeling, assessment exemplars, and rubrics to assist learner performance and improvement.	Feedback is provided on assessments. Teacher uses modeling and rubrics to assist learner performance and improvement. Some assessment exemplars may be provided.	Feedback consists of grades/ points and some evaluative comments. Teacher uses modeling, rubrics and assessment exemplars in a minimal way.	Feedback consists primarily of grades/points.

Appendix 4-B (continued)

RUBRIC FOR HLTP #10: Developing Contextualized Performance Assessments

Use of Assessment Results	Teacher uses assessment results to improve learning and instruction. Teacher provides individual dialogic sessions with learners in a systematic fashion to discuss progress and a plan for improvement.	Teacher uses assessment results to improve learning and instruction. Teacher provides opportunities to discuss progress with individual students and a plan for improvement.	Teacher uses assessment results to discuss progress with the entire class and conduct remediation and/or review.	Teacher uses assessment results primarily to evaluate performance and assign grades.

CHAPTER 5

Putting It Back Together: Embracing and Reconstructing the Practices

Reconstruction is a complement to deconstruction and is a process that can play a pivotal role "in both learning individual core practices and in building a teaching repertoire" (Janssen, Grossman, & Westbroek, 2015, p. 141).

Ten HLTPs have been presented in this two-volume series in view of the need for their successful enactment in foreign language classrooms whose goals include **ambitious teaching**, defined by Troyan, Davin, & Donato as "instructional experiences that support students in carrying out cognitively demanding tasks" (2013, p. 174). These practices are recognized as essential by language teaching professionals and have a theoretical basis and research support in the field of foreign language education. As widely discussed in the larger educational field, HTLPs need to be deconstructed (i.e., decomposed) into smaller instructional moves that can be understood, learned, and practiced by novice teachers. Some researchers have proposed that focusing on the enactment of high-leverage practices would "elevate...the professionalism of teaching and teacher education" (Ball & Forzani, 2009, p. 509). Accordingly, in these two volumes, each practice has been deconstructed into instructional moves made visible to novice teachers and put into practice through rehearsal and self-assessment. The final chapter of the first volume outlines a cycle of enactment to lead teachers through six phases that occur in an iterative fashion:

1. Deconstruction of the HLTP
2. Observation and analysis of the HLTP
3. Planning to enact the practice
4. Rehearsal and coaching
5. Enactment of practice in the PK-16 classroom
6. Assessment of enactment by one or more of the collaborative partners, including self-assessment and reflection (Glisan & Donato, 2017, p. 166).

In the last several years, the ongoing process of identifying and deconstructing high-level practices across disciplines has prompted the need for further clarification regarding the role of the teacher in embracing these practices—i.e., what it takes to enable teachers to enact HLTPs. High-leverage practices are not prescriptions to be followed, nor is the Cycle of Enactment merely a series of linear steps that the teacher checks off in attempting to learn the practices. Instead, HLTPs are fundamental 'building blocks' for novice and in-service teachers to use as they design instruction and engage their students in learning (Janssen, Grossman, & Westbroek, 2015). Further, skill in enacting HLTPs is a developmental process that takes place over time, requires decision making, and is facilitated through coaching and reflection with others (De Arment, Reed, & Wetzel, 2013; Janssen, Grossman, & Westbroek, 2015).

While on the one hand, the goals of ambitious teaching require deconstruction of HLTPs into smaller instructional moves, on the other hand, teachers must also **reconstruct** (i.e., recompose) these practices as they design and execute complete lessons for the unique circumstances of their classrooms (Janssen, Grossman, & Westbroek, 2015). Reconstruction is a complement to deconstruction and is a process that can play a pivotal role "in both learning individual core practices and in building a teaching repertoire" (Janssen, Grossman, & Westbroek, 2015, p. 141). In this regard, this chapter will explore four factors that have been found to be instrumental in prompting teachers to embrace and reconstruct HLTPs:

1. Situating of practices within larger **instructional activities** (IAs) to gain understanding of the function and meaning of the practices. Although each HLTP in this two-volume series has been deconstructed into smaller-grain practices (e.g., paraphrasing to increase the comprehensibility of the target language or specifying learning outcomes as one part of the iterative backward-planning process), to understand and successfully enact HLTPs requires situating each practice in the larger context of an organized, purposeful, and contextualized instructional activity appropriate for the level of the class.
2. Teachers' **will**, or motivation, to enact HLTPs as an important consideration in addition to their knowledge. The willingness to learn how to enact an HLTP successfully is closely associated with the teacher's identity as an education professional who continually seeks to develop and expand pedagogical knowledge and skill.
3. Development of **adaptive expertise**, i.e., the ability to modify and extend the instructional moves previously deconstructed in order to address novel instructional situations and learner needs.
4. Coaching and dialogic reflection.

Each of these factors will be discussed with examples taken from the ten practices for foreign language presented in this two-volume series.

Situating HLTPs within Instructional Activities: Dealing with Complexity

A student teacher enrolled in a peer teaching practicum course stands in front of the class demonstrating her ability to convey meaning in the target language in a comprehensible way. She crumples up a piece of paper into a ball and proceeds to place it in various positions in relation to a book. For each new position, she produces a target language utterance intended to represent what her peers observe – *the ball is under the book, the ball is next to the book, the ball in on the book.* Her peers become restless and bored, and, although her language was somewhat comprehensible, the instructional activity in which the high-leverage practice of using comprehensible language was embedded had no meaning, no purpose, no context, and no clear connection to the learning outcomes of the lesson in which it may have been a part. This scenario illustrates the importance of situating the rehearsal of high-leverage practices in purposeful instructional activities rather than decontextualized and scripted routines, a concept that is explored in more detail below.

A practice-based approach to teacher preparation is based on the idea that teachers need opportunities to rehearse and experiment, with coaching and support, the complex moves that make up HLTPs. In response to the scenario above, the literature on practice-based teacher education stresses the need to ground rehearsal in a specific **instructional activity** that provides a limited space to practice the various instructional moves of an HLTP while simultaneously envisioning its connection to larger lesson goals and learning outcomes. By focusing on the HLTP in a meaningful and contextualized instructional activity rather than as a decontextualized and scripted routine, novices can practice specific pedagogical moves and make decisions about how to interact with their students using the high-leverage practice and based on the overall goals of the activity and lesson (Janssen, Grossman, & Westbroek, 2015; Lampert & Graziani, 2009). Rehearsing the various HLTPs within specific instructional activities gives meaning and purpose to the practice being learned and increases understanding of the role of the HLTP in instruction.

As this two-volume series has shown, understanding an HLTP occurs through a deconstruction of its instructional moves, the hierarchical organization of these moves, and the specific goals of the practice. The individual moves of each HLTP do not exist in isolation, however, and only take on meaning when viewed from the perspective of the practice as a whole within the instructional activities that make up segments of the particular lesson. For example, although determining the setting where a communication may take place is one part of establishing context (HLTP #7), alone it cannot account for a contextualized lesson where students learn that the use of the target language is influenced by a host of factors that are co-present in the setting, including participants, goals of the interaction, and language functions that achieve communicative goals, among other factors. Additionally, contextualizing instruction is not a high-leverage practice that emerges in one disconnected segment of a full lesson or unit. Rather, the high-leverage practice of contextualization is woven into *all* the learning experiences of the lesson/unit, such as introducing new thematic vocabulary related to the topic of the lesson/unit, conducting a dialogic grammar lesson based on a cultural folktale presented in class, or jointly constructing a purposeful written text relevant to the content and context of the lesson/unit.

According to Lampert & Graziani (2009), segments of a full lesson (and also of a unit) are made up of well-sequenced instructional activities (i.e., learning experiences; see HLTP #8). Janssen, Grossman, and Westbroek state that "instructional activities provide a frame, or structured whole, that provides meaning to the individual core practices [HLTPs] that constitute the lesson segments involved" (2015, p. 141). Simply put, instructional activities are learning experiences that make up various segments of a lesson or unit and that address and support learning outcomes. Organizing and sequencing instructional activities within the segments of the lesson shape the lesson as a whole and result in coherent instruction (see HLTP #8). Examples of instructional activities associated with high-leverage practices include a text-based interpretive discussion as one phase of a reading lesson, a co-constructed grammar discussion in a PACE lesson, or an oral interpersonal task based on the theme of the lesson. As these examples illustrate, various instructional moves of the HLTP play critical roles in the instructional activity and can serve as foci for practice and rehearsal, be it asking appropriate and clear questions about a visual during an IMAGE model culture lesson or about a model text during a genre-based presentational writing lesson (for more examples, see Chapter 7, Volume I, Figure 7.1).

HLTPs are complex and need to be deconstructed and the instructional moves made visible to the novice teacher. But simply having knowledge of the various instructional moves of a complex HLTP is not enough. As Janssen, Grossman, and Westbroek point out, "knowledge alone cannot support skillful performance" (2015, p. 137). Rehearsal of HLTPs is necessary to gain control of the practice, to understand how it is integrated it into full lessons and units, and to enact it at a later time in the unpredictable and changing conditions of classroom life. For this reason, when a [student] teacher is engaged in rehearsal, the instructional moves of large-grain HLTPs need to be situated within an activity to make clear the meaning and function of the instructional moves and their contributions to the learning outcomes of the lesson. Rehearsal in the context of an instructional activity may initially focus on *practicing only one instructional move* of the large-grain-size HLTP, e.g., practicing paraphrasing as one discourse move of the larger high-leverage practice of increasing target language comprehensibility, providing feedback to student contributions during the practice of a text-based discussion, or jointly constructing a written text with students as one part of a genre-based presentational writing lesson. The important point is that when practicing and rehearsing one instructional move of a larger-grain-size HLTP, the instructional move can only be understood in the context of an instructional activity that has meaning, purpose, and a goal. The decision to focus on one instructional move of an HLTP in the context of a meaningful instructional activity depends, therefore, on the complexity of the HLTP and the pedagogical skill and teaching experience of the student teachers, university teaching assistants, or in-service teachers. As control of one part of the practice develops (e.g., telling a story in an interactive way in a PACE lesson), rehearsals can be expanded to include other instructional moves of the HLTP (e.g., telling a story followed by conducting a dialogic grammar conversation based on the story). By expanding the HLTP to include additional instructional moves, teachers gain control of the complexity of the larger-grain-size HLTP and move to greater degrees of expertise.

To return to the opening 'paper ball' scenario, how much more effective and useful it would have been if the rehearsal of the high-leverage practice of using language comprehensibly had been situated in an instructional activity dealing with urban life, e.g., describing a visual of the layout of a target language city, identifying the location of well-known landmarks and monuments, or making comparisons between the target language city and the city in which students live. In this way, rehearsing speaking in comprehensible ways (HLTP #1) within a meaningful instructional activity transforms the high-leverage practice of comprehensible target language use during instruction beyond the limited grammar-driven goal of teaching prepositions of location and serves the larger purpose of creating cultural knowledge, increasing student motivation and interest, and fostering a classroom discourse community.

Teachers' Skill and Will

Becoming an accomplished teacher requires more than simply learning how to enact instructional routines and practice. Teachers must also develop a professional identity that welcomes new instructional approaches and their connections to timely educational issues related to teachers' work. How teachers self-identify as professionals is closely linked to their *willingness* to reflect on and analyze their instruction and to improve their instructional *skills*. The will to continue to grow as an educator and refine instructional skills is founded on this sense of self as an inquiring and reflective educational professional (Ronfeldt, 2008).

A strong professional identity mediates the connection of a teacher's will to work toward refining the pedagogical skills necessary for effective instruction. Viewing oneself as a professional fuels the will to sharpen and refine the work of teaching and produces an openness to developing instructional expertise. Without the will to learn and engage with HLTPs, no amount of professional development or repeated cycles of rehearsals will produce a highly skilled teacher who knows how and why the use of HLTPs supports specific instructional goals and the needs of learners. In short, *skill* as a teacher and the *will* to learn and refine the work of instruction are two essential qualities that are at the core of one's professional identity (Donato, 2017).

Professional identity is also intimately connected with teachers' *goals* for the kinds of teachers they want to be, their motivation to learn HLPTs, and their ability to reconstruct HLTPs to meet the demands of their classes (see section below on adaptive expertise). For example, in the context of foreign language education, if a teacher's overarching goal is to become a standards-based, proficiency-oriented instructor, this teacher is more likely to be willing to explore and practice an HLTP that engages students in rich target language conversations in the classroom, includes authentic texts for developing the interpretive mode of communication, and views grammar as a tool for realizing and supporting functional learning outcomes. Conversely, if a teacher's goal is to reduce all innovative ideas to the status of "I do this already" or "This will never work in my class," then this teacher will have little motivation to embrace HLTPs, to rehearse and welcome feedback, and to make changes to instruction where changes are necessary. Janssen, Grossman, and Westbroek (2015) state that teachers will persist in learning to enact and understand a high-leverage practice only if they perceive that the skill will facilitate important professional goals (e.g., the need to improve instructional planning) and if they are open to examining their preconceived ideas and passionately held beliefs (e.g., most foreign language students are academically weak and unmotivated and can only be asked factual comprehension questions). In the absence of a goal-directed professional identity that is founded upon the will to improve, little skill development can occur.

In foreign language classes, **skill** with the target language is also implicitly, and at times explicitly, connected to a teacher's willingness to learn to enact high-leverage practices. In the absence of target language skills at an Advanced level of proficiency as defined in the ACTFL Proficiency Guidelines (ACTFL, 2012), teachers will struggle with the demands of the practice that requires, for example, tailoring language to the level of the class during discussion (HLTP #1) or analyzing a genre to teach its purpose, cultural content, and functional language features (rather than just salient grammatical forms) (HLTP #9). Refusing to engage with an HLTP may be a way to save face or to avoid the realization that improving language proficiency is necessary. The important point is that developing pedagogical skill does not happen simply by gaining control of a list of teaching strategies and instructional procedures and routines. The ability to use the target language flexibly for instruction at Advanced levels of proficiency is also essential for learning the HLTP and for making the target language accessible to learners across all aspects of instruction (Grossman, Schoenfeld, & Lee, 2005).

Anthony (2018) claims that enacting practice-based teacher education requires courageous teachers who have the will to improve their skill in a collaborative community of professional practice. This community needs to be made up of teachers whose professional identity embraces a spirit of inquiry into instruction, a willingness to share thoughts with colleagues and welcome feedback, and a commitment to the continuous improvement of their practice. Successful practiced-based teacher education and professional development programs go beyond the learning of prescriptions and routines. They require a particular set of teacher dispositions that encourage analysis of instruction, a professional identity consistent with other professions that routinely seek advances in knowledge and skill, and the ability to question professional goals and their relationship to high-leverage practices and quality foreign language education for all students. In summary, skill and will, as they have been explained, are fundamental to professional identity and are essential for creating teachers who seek to develop adaptive expertise, the topic of the next section of this chapter.

Developing Adaptive Expertise

As mentioned earlier, to make ambitious teaching learnable, complex teaching practices are deconstructed into smaller instructional moves that specify the necessary knowledge and skills required to enact them. However, the goal of practice-based teacher education is not to produce 'cookie cutter' teachers who can enact routinized practices, but rather to equip teachers with the understanding and skills to enact HLTPs and be able to adapt and extend these routines depending on their students' needs and instructional contexts. In this vein, it is seldom appropriate to enact a practice using the same predetermined steps every time, given the complex interactions of the classroom and novel learning situations. Hence, research on practice-based teacher education is focusing not only on the enactment of instructional routines but also on the development of **adaptive expertise**, that is, the ability of teachers to "adapt and extend their routines, by accepting new possibilities or attempting to solve old problems in different ways" (Janssen, Grossman, & Westbroek, 2015, p. 139). Further, adaptive expertise has been called the "gold standard for becoming a professional" (Hammerness, Darling-Hammond, & Bransford, 2005, p. 360).

Teachers develop skill in adapting HLTPs as these practices become more *automatic* and *internalized*; as some aspects of a practice become more automatic, teachers are freed up to think about how other aspects can be changed or extended to address novel teaching situations or learner needs (Janssen, Grossman, & Westbroek, 2015). In this regard, an important goal for professional development is to provide ample opportunities for novice teachers to rehearse the HLTPs so that the practices become more automatic and internalized over time, thus providing space for adaptive expertise to develop. Undoubtedly some knowledge of and experience in enacting new practices is necessary before adaptation can occur successfully. As Jenkins states, "...learn how to do something in the time-tested, traditional way and then, as you become more adept, start to add your own flair" (2020, p. 3). To this end, research suggests that novice teachers can develop skill in enacting HLTPs in a routinized manner while also expanding their teaching repertoire by adapting certain aspects of these practices (De Arment, Reed, & Wetzel, 2013; Janssen, Grossman, & Westbroek, 2015). Bransford, Derry, Berliner, and Hammerness suggest a process in which teachers are guided and coached to become both "routine experts" and "adaptive experts." They frame adaptive expertise as a balance between "efficiency" in enacting routinized HTLPs and "innovation" (including experimentation) in adapting these practices (2005, p. 49). However, as Janssen, Grossman, and Westbroek state, "The challenge is to find the right balance between both processes. Too much emphasis on innovation will probably lead to frustrated novices. Sole focus on developing routines will lead to routine experts" (2013, p. 144).

The development of adaptive expertise involves critical thinking, flexibility, and problem-solving skills as teachers consider the benefits of adapting elements of a practice when faced with ever-changing instructional situations and challenges within the classroom (see, for example, De Arment, Reed, and Wetzel, 2013). As discussed earlier in this chapter, teachers' dispositional characteristics and professional identities are also pivotal in this process, particularly their will to engage in self-reflection and instructional improvement, and to view their assumptions about learning in a dynamic, rather than static, manner. To this end, teachers are constantly self-assessing and reflecting as they make decisions about whether to use a routinized practice as is or adapt it. In fact, an **inquiry stance** is a key attribute of adaptive expertise and ultimately enables teachers to shift their focus from self to student by putting themselves in the roles of their learners; i.e., they "become students of their students and learners of their own practice" (Anthony, 2018, p. 7). In this regard, adaptive experts are willing to take risks in trying out novel instructional moves as additions to routinized practices, and they seek out feedback and coaching from others.

Decision-Making as Adaptive Expertise

A critical aspect of adaptive expertise is decision making. Enacting HLTPs is not a mindless linear deconstruction of practices but rather involves decision-making. Throughout Volume I and this volume, we have stressed the role of the teacher as decision maker, both in planning instruction and in enacting the practices in a moment-by-moment fashion in the classroom. In fact, all of the practices presented in these two volumes have built into them the need for the teacher to use adaptive expertise. The various mediational tools provide scaffolded options for the teacher to consider while taking into account the specific instructional context and learner needs. Below are several examples of how the teacher develops adaptive expertise while working on enacting the routinized practices.

1. In facilitating target language comprehensibility (HLTP #1, Volume I), the teacher decides in advance which contexts will be used to create an instructional activity with a purpose that is relevant to learners' lives and what types of interactions will illustrate learner comprehension. As the activity unfolds, the teacher decides how to make language comprehensible by choosing paraphrases or definitions, by slowing down the rate of speech, or by signaling new words and structures with tone of voice.

2. In designing oral interpersonal tasks between pairs of students (HLTP #2—Part 2, Volume I), the teacher decides which instructional activity would best represent the theme and objectives of instruction while prompting students to use communicative strategies to communicate meaningful messages. Additionally, the teacher makes decisions about how to manage the instructional activity—how to group

students, how much time to allow for the task, and what students will do as a follow-up after the task.

3. In focusing on form in a dialogic context through PACE (HLTP #4, Volume I), the teacher chooses from many options the type of story to tell in the P phase and how comprehension will be checked. In the C phase, if learners are unable to co-construct the grammatical form initially, the teacher must decide how to proceed—that is, go back to the story, provide additional clues, or try another strategy.
4. In providing oral corrective feedback (HLTP #6, Volume I) during a discussion of a cultural infographic, the teacher uses the decision-making tool to make on-the-spot decisions about the type of corrective feedback to provide or whether to provide corrective feedback at all.
5. In planning for instruction (HLTP #8, Volume II), the teacher uses the planning tool in an iterative fashion as decisions are made as to whether it is necessary to return to earlier stages of the backward-design process to make adjustments to the plan as it evolves.
6. In engaging learners in purposeful written communication (HLTP #9, Volume II), the teacher selects a model text at an appropriate level and length for the class, analyzes the genre, and decides how the text will be described in student-friendly language to her class.

Beyond the types of decisions that are a part of enacting these practices, teachers might also develop adaptive expertise by experimenting with some of the instructional moves for specific practices and adapting and extending them in innovative ways to meet new instructional challenges. A caveat, however, is that teachers must justify adaptations using the research and theoretical base that supports the practice, as opposed to making random adaptations that might not be supported by research. For example, in focusing on form in a dialogic context through PACE (HLTP #4, Volume I), the teacher might adapt the P phase by telling a story and showing a video without sound instead of using photos or props—this adaptation is innovative yet still supports the theoretical basis for the PACE Approach. An adaptation that would not be supported by the PACE research base would be to provide an English translation of the PACE story or to read the story aloud in the absence of visual support.

Considerations on and Strategies for Developing Adaptive Expertise in Teachers

Although adaptive expertise is a goal in practice-based teacher education, helping teachers to develop this skill can be challenging, mostly because it requires dialogic interaction with peers, coaching and mediation by experts, and time to engage in self-reflection and instructional improvement. The important role of coaching in learning to enact HLTPs was explained in Chapter 7 of Volume I. Coaching has an even more pivotal role in developing adaptive expertise, and, in fact, it is unlikely that adaptive expertise can develop without it. The process of coaching involves moment-to-moment mediation and guidance as a teaching enactment unfolds; this procedure is commonplace in many professional communities, such as learning to be a physician or pilot. Unfortunately, we have a long way to go in the foreign language profession before students and mentors are comfortable with coaching as an integral part of a teacher education program (Glisan & Donato, 2017, p. 170; Troyan, Davin, & Donato, 2013).

In addition to a coach who is present for teaching performances, mediation and support can also be provided by a **dialogic partner**—i.e., an individual who can serve as a "sympathetic other" or person with whom experiences, views, feelings, and ideas can be shared and discussed in a non-threatening space (Brooks, 2002, p. 82). Dialogic partnerships are extremely helpful for in-service teachers (including student teachers and interns), who are often isolated and must function in the absence of a class of peers and a professor to offer ongoing support. In this vein, Brooks (2002), a university language methods course instructor, returned to the elementary school classroom to teach Spanish to fifth graders and to test out his theories about language learning and teaching against the reality of teaching 'real' learners. A key feature of his study was the dialogic partnership that he developed with a colleague from a different university, who served as his sympathetic other in helping him to make sense of his experience. Brooks sums up his experience with a recommendation to student interns:

> ...I will encourage student interns to seek out others with whom they can engage in professional conversations about their work. There is a certain sense of loneliness in being constrained from connecting with other professionals. It is important to share views, experiences, feelings, and ideas, to explore reasons why an instructional event did or did not seem to work. Involvement in the dialogic partnership with my colleague proved invaluable and was a tremendous support mechanism for me. Wrapped up in the daily issues that I experienced at the school, my dialogue allowed me to construct ideas and seek collaboration with an equally interested educator. In some ways it allowed me to vent to a sympathetic other who was in a different environment and thus removed from it all. (2002, p. 82)

In teacher education programs at the college or university level, in which there are opportunities to mentor and coach pre-service teachers, space can be provided within methods courses and practicum experiences for adaptive expertise to develop. First, novices can watch expert teachers enact HLTPs, identifying the adaptations made by the expert. This activity can be followed by a discussion among novices that is mediated by the professor or supervisor. Secondly, once novices have demonstrated skill in enacting a particular practice, the professor or supervisor might introduce a 'what-if scenario' that would prompt an adaptation (Lin, Schwartz, & Bransford, 2007). For example, in focusing on cultural products, practices, and perspectives in a dialogic context using the IMAGE Model (HLTP #5, Volume I), novices might be asked what they would do if their learners were unsure as to how to respond to a specific thought question in the target language. Thirdly, after novices have gained experience in enacting a specific practice, they could be asked to introduce an adaptation to the practice and justify it based on learner needs and with research and theoretical considerations that support the adaptation. These adaptations could be presented to a methods or practicum class and could serve as the basis of a mediated discussion. Finally, research evidence indicates that novices benefit from enacting practices in a variety of instructional contexts in which adaptations would likely be necessary (De Arment, Reed, & Wetzel, 2013). In this regard, education programs should make every attempt to provide classroom experiences in diverse instructional settings in which HLTPs can be enacted.

The ideas presented above assume that the supervisor/professor serves the role of a dialogic partner and supportive coach, which is a critical factor in helping novices to improve their ability to adapt practices, as discussed above. Studies have shown that a 'guiding and reflecting' supervision style, when compared with a 'telling' supervision style, encourages novices to engage in discussion about the problems they face in developing adaptive teaching expertise (Soslau, 2012; cf. De Arment, Reed, & Wetzel, 2013, p. 10). Arguably, many professors and supervisors are likely to need training themselves in how to coach teachers-in-training and provide supportive scaffolding and mediation so that novices have safe spaces in which to develop the ability to experiment, adapt, and innovate within the HLTP frameworks. In this regard, several recent studies have examined the capacity of teacher educators to engage in practice-based work. For example, Peercy and Troyan's (2017) research suggests that teacher educators may need to make both conceptual and practical shifts as they learn how to interact with novice teachers in enacting HLTPs. More specifically, Peercy and Troyan (2020) argue for a process that promotes greater collaboration and participation between teacher educators and novice teachers, so that pedagogy avoids focusing on the 'expert' and instead aligns with sociocultural perspectives on learning. Clearly, additional research is needed to document the journey of teacher educators as they strive to embrace practice-based approaches to teacher education.

Developing adaptive expertise among in-service teachers is a much more daunting endeavor inasmuch as most teachers lack both time for reflection during the day and support from fellow teachers or mentors. As one possibility, a group of teachers could form a community of practice and engage in 'lesson study' in which they observe and work with one another to support the development of adaptive expertise in their classes (Lewis & Hurd, 2011). Ideally, teachers would have ongoing professional development opportunities that build in opportunities for coaching, dialogue, and mediation to occur over time. However, the current reality is that few school districts have the resources to provide the type of support that teachers need to become adaptive experts, and even in some cases to become experts at enacting the ten practices presented in these two volumes. When we reflect on this situation more deeply, we wonder if the 'resources are lacking' argument is really nothing more than an excuse to cover the sad fact that many administrators (and maybe even teachers?) do not understand or value the pivotal role of coaching and dialogic partnerships, perhaps because they represent a new approach for foreign language preparation and professional development that is just too daunting. Anecdotally speaking, many professionals still prefer to remain in the comfort of a system that is familiar to them, even if it no longer serves the needs of the teaching community. Perhaps in the larger picture, the value of HLTPs and practice-based teacher education lies in prompting the profession to recognize what is lacking in order to move forward in ways that truly enable teachers to embrace HLTPs and develop adaptive expertise. The language teaching profession is facing a stark reality: It is at a crossroads where it must decide whether or not to take advantage of the challenge that HLTPs present in order to leverage not only classroom language instruction but also teacher professional development.

References

American Council on the Teaching of Foreign Languages (ACTFL). (2012). *ACTFL proficiency guidelines.* Alexandria, VA: Author. Retrieved from https://www.actfl.org/publications/guidelines-and-manuals/actfl-proficiency-guidelines-2012

Anthony, G. (2018). Practice-based teacher education: Developing inquiring professionals. In G. Kaiser, H. Forgasz, M. Graven, A. Kuzniak, E. Simmt, & B. Xu (Eds.), *Invited lectures from the 13th International Congress on Mathematical Education.* ICME-13 Monographs (pp. 1-18). doi: 10.1007/978-3-319-72170-5 1

Ball, D. L., & Forzani, F. M. (2009). The work of teaching and the challenge for teacher education. *Journal of Teacher Education, 60*(5), 497-511.

Bransford, J., Derry, S., Berliner, D., & Hammerness, K. (2005). Introduction. In L. Darling-Hammond & J. Bransford (Eds.), *Preparing teachers for a changing world: What teachers should learn and be able to do* (pp. 1-39). San Francisco: Jossey-Bass.

Brooks, F. B. (2002). My theory is intact; however,...: Teaching Spanish to fifth graders. *Foreign Language Annals, 35,* 73-84.

De Arment, S. T., Reed, E., & Wetzel, A. P. (2013). Promoting adaptive expertise: A conceptual framework for special educator preparation. *Teacher Education and Special Education: The Journal of the Teacher Education Division of the Council for Exceptional Children.* Retrieved from http://tes.sagepub.com/content/early/2013/06/20/0888406413489578

Donato, R. (2017). Becoming a language teaching professional: What's identity got to do with it? In G. Barkhuizen (Ed.), *Reflections on language teacher identity research* (pp. 24-30). New York: Routledge.

Glisan, E. W., & Donato, R. (2017). *Enacting the work of language instruction: High-leverage teaching practices.* Alexandria, VA: ACTFL.

Grossman, P, Schoenfeld, A., & Lee, C. (2005). Teaching subject matter. In L. Darling-Hammond & J. Bransford (Eds.), *Preparing teachers for a changing world: What teachers should learn and be able to do* (pp. 201-231). San Francisco: Jossey-Bass.

Hammerness, K., Darling-Hammond, L., & Bransford, J. (2005). How teachers learn and develop. In L. Darling-Hammond & J. Bransford (Eds.), *Preparing teachers for a changing world: What teachers should learn and be able to do* (pp. 358-389). San Francisco: Jossey-Bass.

Janssen, F., Grossman, P., & Westbroek, H. (2015). Facilitating decomposition and recomposition in practice-based teacher education: The power of modularity. *Teaching and Teacher Education, 51,* 137-146.

Jenkins, R. (2020). Why we must get back to basics in teaching composition. *The Chronicle of Higher Education.* Retrieved from https://chroniclevitae.com/news/2300-why-we-must-get-back-to-basics-in-teaching-composition

Lampert, M., & Graziani, F. (2009). Instructional activities as a tool for teachers' and teacher educators' learning. *Elementary School Journal, 109*(5), 491-509.

Lewis, C. C., & Hurd, J. (2011). *Lesson study step by step: How teacher learning communities improve instruction.* Portsmouth, NH: Heinemann.

Lin, X., Schwartz, D. L., & Bransford, J. (2007). Intercultural adaptive expertise: Explicit and implicit lessons from Dr. Hatano. *Human Development, 50,* 65-72.

Peercy, M. M., & Troyan, F. J. (2017). Making transparent the challenges of developing a practice-based pedagogy of teacher education. *Teaching and Teacher Education, 61,* 26–36. doi: 10.1016/j.tate.2016.10.005

Peercy, M. M., & Troyan, F. J. (2020). 'Am I doing it right?': Critically examining mediation in lesson rehearsal. *Teaching and Teacher Education, 93.* doi: 10.1016/j.tate.2020.103082

Ronfeldt, M. (2008). *Crafting core selves during professional education.* Stanford, CA: Stanford University.

Soslau, E. (2012). Opportunities to develop adaptive teaching expertise during supervisory conferences. *Teaching and Teacher Education, 28,* 768-779.

Troyan, F. J., Davin, K. J., & Donato, R. (2013). Exploring a practice-based approach to foreign language teacher preparation: A work in progress. *Canadian Modern Language Review/La revue canadienne des langues vivantes, 69,* 154-180.

Made in United States
Cleveland, OH
29 December 2025